YOU
CAN
DO IT!

YOU CAN DO IT!

A Teen's Guide to Developing Strength and Purpose

Daisaku Ikeda

World Tribune
Press

Published by
World Tribune Press
A division of the SGI-USA
606 Wilshire Blvd.
Santa Monica, CA 90401

© 2019 Soka Gakkai

Cover and interior design by Lightbourne, Inc.

23 22 21 20 19   2 3 4 5 6

ISBN: 978-1-944604-25-7
Library of Congress Control Number: 2018949013

CREDITS: 123rf.com: T. Cundrawan, pp. i, iii. Danylo Honchar, pp. 11, 18, 26, 46, 73, 103, 171, 189. Teeranai Nhusricharoen, p. 13. CarlacDesign, pp. 14, 197, 205. Ekaterina Shmachkova, p. 26. Luisa Vallon Fumi, p. 42. Vasilkovs, pp. 43, 52. Sergey Nivens, p. 53. Blue67, pp. 60, 79, 87, 92, 147, 149, 154, 177, 191. Frank Ramspott, pp. 61, 71. Iana Zyrianova, p. 62. Gabriel Colaco, p. 64. Maryia Kryvaltsevich, pp. 66, 203. Marina Zlochin, pp. 68, 76, 93, 99. Ekaterina Arkhangelskaia, p. 70. Pinkpueblo, pp. 75, 129. Ivan Aleshin, p. 95. Drawlab19, pp. 115, 215. Konstantin Kozulko, p. 142. Gmast3r, p. 168. **Alamy Stock Photo:** Ian Dagnall Computing, p. 6. Everett Collection Inc., p. 37. INTERFOTO, p. 55. GL Archive, p. 143. Keystone Pictures, p. 157. DPA Picture Alliance, p. 169. The Advertising Archives, p. 173. Sputnik, p. 212. Album, p. 220. **Ed Chen:** p. 188. **Alex FaiChan:** p. 15. **Getty Images:** Don Cravens, The LIFE Images Collection, p. 113. Gianluigi Guercia, AFP, p. 182. **Ikeda Center for Peace, Learning, and Dialogue:** p. 164. Quote: Elise Boulding and Daisaku Ikeda, *Into Full Flower: Making Peace Cultures Happen* (Cambridge, MA: Dialogue Path Press, 2010), 21. **iStockPhoto:** Nosyrevy, pp. ii, iii, 168. Shiffarigum, pp. v, vii, 1, 2, 4, 11, 31, 35, 41, 51, 68, 123, 141, 145, 225. John Woodcock, p. viii. Palto, pp. 2, 3. Paket, pp. 3, 4, 14, 40, 41, 43, 47, 49, 52, 69, 111, 117, 118, 133. Frank Ramspott, pp. 10, 34, 48, 51, 121, 193. Martin Hosmart, pp. 16. CSA Printstock, p. 19. A-Digit, p. 20. Darijashka, pp. 21, 25. Seb_ra, p. 24. THEPALMER, p. 28. Polygraphus, p. 29. Intueri, p. 39. Arkadivna, p. 50. ONYXprj, pp. 50, 72, 131. Johan10, p. 74. Franckreporter, p. 80. LEOcrafts, p. 81. SlothAstronaut, pp. 89, 101. Wundervisuals, p. 90. SPmemory, p. 110. Frimages, pp. 120, 139. Benjavisa, p. 125. Chipstudio, p. 140. Scottir1, p. 148. HstrongART, p. 158. H2O Color, p. 159. AleksandraKuzmina, p. 163. Handini Atmodiwiryo, p. 166. RYGERSZEM, p. 178. Blue67, p. 179. Terriana, p. 187. Acrylik, p. 194. Nikiteev Konstantin, p. 197. LokFung, p. 206. YummySuperStar, p. 207. Magnilion, p. 216. Peshkova, p. 224. **Masterfile Corporation:** p. 59. **PixtaStock.com:** Itake, p. 30. **Seikyo Press:** pp. 3, 5, 32, 44, 63, 82, 108, 116, 161, 185, 202. **Jonathan Wilson:** p. 84.

CONTENTS

EDITOR'S NOTE

*Y*ou Can Do It! was originally serialized in *Future Journal*, the newspaper for the Soka Gakkai's junior high and high school divisions in Japan, from May 2012 to March 2014 under the title "Dialogue for the Future."

The citations most commonly used in this book have been abbreviated as follows:

OTT, page number(s) refers to *The Record of the Orally Transmitted Teachings*, translated by Burton Watson (Tokyo: Soka Gakkai, 2004).

WND, page number(s) refers to *The Writings of Nichiren Daishonin*, vol. 1 (WND-1) (Tokyo: Soka Gakkai, 1999) and vol. 2 (WND-2) (Tokyo: Soka Gakkai, 2006).

1

Let's Go Forward
TOGETHER ·········>

President Ikeda: I am very happy to have the opportunity
to take part in this series. Through this dialogue I hope to
speak directly with you, young readers, for whom I have
the greatest trust and hopes. [This dialogue was originally
serialized in the *Future Journal,* the Soka Gakkai's monthly
newspaper for junior high and high school students in
Japan.]

I receive many letters from throughout Japan and the
world every day. They include reports on various activities
and members' personal updates. They also include letters
from scholars and leaders in various spheres of society. I
am also engaged in several ongoing dialogues.

But what gives me the greatest joy above all is witnessing
your vibrant growth and earnest efforts. Nothing is more
dazzling than your burgeoning young lives.

Of course, sometimes despite all you do, things may
not go as planned. But always trying your best is itself truly
wonderful.

Though you may not realize this, all of life is a

struggle. Your body, for instance, is comprised of count-less cells, and they all do their utmost to fulfill their functions. They battle to protect you from all sorts of germs and microbes. That's what enables you to keep growing day after day.

Nichiren Buddhism exists for those who want to get the most out of life. Its purpose is to enable all people to live their lives to the fullest and to become happy. The purpose of our Buddhist practice is to win. My role, too, is to ensure that you can all win in life.

Nichiren Buddhism exists for those who want to get the most out of life.

If I could, I'd like to go out right now to meet and talk with each one of you in person. I'd like to sit down with you and share your problems and concerns. It is my wish to do anything I possibly can to encourage and support you, my most precious young friends.

I would like to talk with you as if we were having a leisurely conversation in a beautiful green park somewhere. In that spirit, let's begin our "discussions."

Future Journal: *Junior high and high school students have all sorts of worries—about their studies and future careers, their relations with classmates and teachers, their personality or physical appearance, their parents, and so forth. The severe economic recession seriously impacts many families. And, bullying, even cyberbullying, remains a chronic problem among teenagers.*

President Ikeda: We live in complex times, and the problems we face are truly challenging. It's a very different world from when I was in my teens. No matter what I'm doing, I'm always thinking about you, my young friends, wondering how you are and whether you're okay.

Daisaku Ikeda and historian Arnold Toynbee in the early 1970s. Their dialogue was later published as *Choose Life*.

Forty years ago, I spoke at length with the eminent British historian Arnold Toynbee. He was in his eighties at the time, but he said he always thought about things in terms of what the world of his great-grandchildren would be like. He also said with a smile that striving for the sake of a better future is the secret to staying young.

I'm now [in 2012] around the same age that Professor Toynbee was then, and I really understand how he felt. I would also like to learn a great deal from all of you and to walk toward the future together with you.

History and the wisdom of great thinkers of the past can serve as important guides.

They can be a source of inspiration for pondering the future and making it better and brighter. In this book, therefore, I would like to share with you the treasures of the human spirit I have come across in my reading and travels. I'd like to pass on the priceless treasures of the heart I have gained through my own personal life struggles.

In particular, I was most fortunate in my youth to have been a student of "Toda University." I received instruction from my mentor in life—the second Soka Gakkai president, Josei Toda—each morning on a wide range of subjects. Mr. Toda was an incredibly strict and demanding teacher. He was always asking me, "Daisaku, what book are you reading now?" And with each book we studied, he would delve deeply into the ideas expressed and share his thoughts with me. All of it was invaluable training. That experience is my most prized treasure, and I'd like to pass on to you everything I've learned.

FJ: *In the aftermath of the devastating March 2011 earthquake and tsunami here in Japan, in particular, there is a renewed appreciation of the power of words to inspire people to work together to rebuild their lives and communities.*

President Ikeda: Yes, words have a tremendous power.

I know there are many junior high and high school division members throughout Tohoku who were affected by the disaster. In a circle of mutual encouragement with family, friends, fellow members, and others in their communities, they continue to bravely challenge their difficulties. Despite their terrible ordeal, many have

Soka Gakkai young men who grew up in the Tohoku region volunteer to help clean up the debris in the aftermath of the quake and tsunami, April 2011.

shared their experiences and feelings, and reached out to support and encourage others. They are moving forward, determined not to be defeated. I am proud of them. I want to commend each one of them.

Sometimes in life, events are so shocking we cannot speak. Or we are racked by personal problems so painful that words cannot describe them. But if we nevertheless try, even if just a little, to share our feelings with someone who understands and cares, we will begin to see a glimmer of light. Then we can find our way through. Words really have the power to forge heart-to-heart bonds.

We are traveling a path of victory together. I am not traveling this path alone, nor am I telling you to travel it alone either. It's a journey we are making together. You are moving toward victory together with me, as well as with your good friends and fellow members, one step at a time.

With that in mind, I have chosen some lines from Walt Whitman's poem "Song of the Open Road" to share with you. The poem might be a bit difficult to understand in places, but it's one of my favorites.

Afoot and light-hearted
*   I take to the open road,*
Healthy, free, the world before me,
The long brown path before me
*   leading wherever I choose.*

Henceforth I ask not good-fortune,
*   I myself am good-fortune,*
Henceforth I whimper no more,
*   postpone no more, need nothing,*

Walt Whitman

*Done with indoor complaints, libraries, querulous
   criticisms,*
Strong and content I travel the open road.[1]

The title, "Song of the Open Road," itself is wonderful.
It's so uplifting and positive. Your futures, too, are like the
road in this poem—open and filled with boundless possibility. No one can stand in your way or hold you back.

I first read this poem at age nineteen, soon after I met
Mr. Toda. I was a little older than you are now. I spent
my youth in the turbulent period following World War II.
After the war, many of the values we had been taught at
school in Japan during the militarist era were demolished.
We young people felt like we could no longer believe in
anything.

When the war ended, none of us knew what to do with
our lives. There was nothing secure to hold on to. In addition, I had tuberculosis, and the doctor said I probably
wouldn't live to age thirty. In the evenings, I'd always have
a low-grade fever. Every day was extremely difficult. I was
exhausted both physically and spiritually. The only things I
could turn to for support were books.

But books were difficult to come by in those days. This
may be hard to imagine, but when you wanted a book,
you had to line up for hours in front of the bookstore.
Even then you might not be able to buy a copy. Whitman's
collection of poems, **Leaves of Grass**, which I purchased at
that time, was a real treasure for me. In it, I read "Song of
the Open Road," and I memorized the parts that resonated

with me. Whenever I recited them, I felt as if the great poet's spirit was alive within me. That is how I encouraged myself and lifted my spirits.

Mr. Toda taught me, a young man searching to find his way, the supreme path of life. After meeting him at nineteen, I joined my mentor on his free, untrammeled journey along that great road.

Like the lines of Whitman's poem said, I myself was "good-fortune." I was deeply happy. I needed nothing else. The road that Mr. Toda had been traveling became my road. As his disciple, I fought and I won. And I still continue to walk that road today. I have not a single regret.

> "Henceforth I ask not good-fortune, **I myself am good-fortune.**"
> —Whitman

FJ: *There are some other inspiring lines from "Song of the Open Road" that you have shared at various times, urging us to press onward toward our goal not bothered by struggles along the way:*

Allons! through struggles and wars!
The goal that was named cannot be countermanded.[2]

President Ikeda: These words are also an important treasure, which I have shared with many young people over the years.

Life is full of struggles and challenges. But all of you are destined to win and become happy without fail. No one can take away your true goal or purpose in life. When facing a series of difficult challenges, the way to break through them is to keep going bravely straight ahead. That is the quickest, most direct route to victory.

There will be times when you struggle and have problems. But that is proof that you are moving along the path of victory. There may be times when you come to a temporary standstill and feel too discouraged or exhausted to continue. When that happens, just take a deep breath and set out once more when you feel ready. Remember, we are always together, sharing the journey.

Since challenges are unavoidable in life, we might as well make our way with a joyful, positive spirit. That has been my attitude. No matter what criticism or abuse was directed at me, I never retreated a single step. This is because I am the disciple of the lionhearted Josei Toda.

Whitman also had good friends and companions. One of them was his physician, Sir William Osler, a pioneer of modern medicine. Osler wrote, "Courage and cheerfulness will not only carry you over the rough places of life, but will enable you to bring comfort and help to the weak-hearted."[3]

By overcoming your challenges and problems with "courage and cheerfulness," you can encourage and inspire many others.

It will soon be your time to take the stage. You all have your own destination. You may not know what it is yet. Or maybe you can't see the meaning of the efforts you are making now. But as long as you keep trying and doing your best to move forward, your destination will definitely come into focus. Each of you undoubtedly has a purpose and mission that is yours and yours alone.

Let's set out on a journey together! I'm with you all the way. I am chanting for you every day. Let's together travel the open road of victory to our destination, with confidence, joy, and a song in our heart.

Let Your Unique Personality SHINE!

Future Journal: *We have received many enthusiastic emails and letters in response to the start of this series from students.*

President Ikeda: I'm happy to hear that. Thank you!

This dialogue is a joint effort with you, the readers of the *Future Journal*. You are my all-important partners. And since our theme is the future, you are the main focus. Let's talk freely about whatever you like.

FJ: *In their emails and letters, many wrote saying that they were worried about their personality. Here are some of the things they wrote: "I'm very quiet and serious, and find it difficult to make friends," "I don't like myself," and "How can I change my personality?"*

President Ikeda: Having problems and worries means you're growing. Because you're moving forward, you're bound to come up against obstacles now and then. I thank these young readers for sharing their feelings so honestly.

There are times in our youth when we feel like we're just a jumble of imperfections. When I was young, I also worried a great deal about my personality and tried to improve it.

You're all at an impressionable age right now, so it is only natural that you'll have such worries. But if you try to be someone you're not, you'll only exhaust yourself. Please bear in mind that personality refers to a person's unique traits. It has nothing to do with people's intrinsic worth. I hope you'll always remember that.

And when you think about it, is there such a thing as a good personality or a bad one? Is it bad to be timid? If everyone were assertive, the arguing would never stop! What about being quiet? If everyone were talkative, how could we stand the noise? It takes all kinds of people— vivacious, chatty people, people who listen quietly and intently, people who don't say a lot but whose every word is worth its weight in gold. Many people find it difficult to speak in public or feel nervous when meeting someone new. I laud those who summon up their courage and overcome their nervousness.

If you think being quiet and serious is a problem, perhaps you could describe yourself instead as "thoughtful," "calm and composed," or "level-headed and collected." You will no doubt find good friends who trust and appreciate you for those qualities. And you'll also be able to trust and appreciate them for theirs.

If you really try, you can change all the shortcomings you see into strengths—especially when you work toward a goal bigger than yourself. Then you can make positive and valuable use of your unique traits in a way that is true to yourself.

FJ: *Some readers have written that they feel like they're always altering their personalities to fit in with their friends, or that they don't know how to act at school and feel different from everyone else.*

President Ikeda: Just be yourself. Buddhism likens people's personalities to the flowers of the cherry, plum, peach, and damson. It teaches that each, though different and unique, is beautiful just as it is.

Buddhism teaches that each, though different and unique, *is beautiful just as it is.*

Being sensitive to those around you is, in a way, a sign of someone who is considerate of others. You can develop such consideration into a fine strong point.

Feeling different from everyone else means that you have your own path. You don't want to be clueless, as the saying goes, or oblivious to the situation or the mood of those around you. On the other hand, you'll exhaust yourself if you spend all your time and energy focused on what everyone else is thinking. As you gain experience, you'll enjoy learning how to communicate well and how to respond appropriately to what's going on. Have confidence in yourself and accept yourself for who you are. Don't worry too much about what others think.

These days, with cell phones and the internet, we are all connected to many more people than we were in the past. As junior high and high school students, you must be bombarded daily with huge amounts of information and differing opinions. But you mustn't let others define you. The answers to your questions are inside you. I hope that, through self-searching and reflection, you will unearth the wonderful qualities that are your own treasures. If you work to develop your strong points, then even traits that you consider to be flaws or weaknesses will come to shine.

I'd like to share with you a quote from *Musashi*, a novel I read in my youth: "Instead of wanting to be like this or that, make yourself into a silent, immovable giant. That's what the mountain is."[4]

FJ: **Musashi** *was written by the Japanese novelist Eiji Yoshikawa. The novel's hero, the master swordsman*

Miyamoto Musashi, says these words to his young successor as they look at Mount Fuji in the distance.

President Ikeda: My fifth and sixth grade homeroom teacher, Kohei Hiyama, read it aloud in class. I still remember with delight how he would enthusiastically act it out. Yoshikawa depicted Musashi as perfecting himself through the way of swordsmanship. Musashi's unswerving dedication to his path, despite many obstacles and setbacks, inspired many readers.

Mr. Toda was also fond of this novel. Along with his mentor, Tsunesaburo Makiguchi,

Miyamoto Musashi

Mr. Toda remained steady in his Buddhist practice and beliefs throughout the growing Japanese militarism that eventually led Japan into World War II. Harassment and persecution by the state authorities could not deter him in his struggle to protect the correct teaching of Nichiren Buddhism. As a result, he was unjustly imprisoned.

In fact, among the things Mr. Toda requested to be sent to him in prison was a copy of **Musashi**. Even in the hellish conditions of prison in wartime Japan, Mr. Toda retained a strong, unflinching spirit, as resolute as Mount Fuji. He never compromised his beliefs. In the stifling heat of summer and the bitter cold of winter, he continued to chant Nam-myoho-renge-kyo in his solitary cell. After the war, he inherited the spiritual legacy and vision of Mr. Makiguchi, who had died in prison. Toda then began his struggle for the happiness of humanity and world peace.

If I were to describe Mr. Toda's greatness in a single phrase, I would say he was a man of powerful conviction. No matter how harsh the circumstances, he was always fearless and self-confident. That's why he could reassure and give courage to others. He was a great leader. He was an indomitable champion.

It's important to build a self as solid as Mount Fuji—a self that will remain unshaken and unswayed by negative remarks or suffering. This is the key to winning in life. And faith in the Mystic Law is the ultimate source for developing such inner strength.

It's almost inevitable when you're young to sometimes feel that others are better than you or have qualities you

wish you had. Comparing yourself to others isn't necessarily bad. When you see someone admirable, you may aspire to emulate them. If that motivates you to improve yourself, it's a good thing. But you shouldn't be impatient. There's no need to rush. Take the time to grow and develop yourself. Things that are easy to build are likely to crumble just as easily. Construction is a difficult, all-out struggle.

Mr. Toda said to young people: "There's no need to put yourself down. You don't need to go to unreasonable lengths to try to change the way you are either. If you persevere in your Buddhist practice, the very character traits you now find so troubling will quite naturally turn into virtues. Live with confidence and be true to yourself."

LIVE WITH CONFIDENCE and be true to yourself.

FJ: More and more young people nowadays seem to lack confidence in themselves.

President Ikeda: I think this all comes back to young people's insecurities about their personalities. But they shouldn't worry. No one starts out full of confidence.

From childhood, I was physically weak, and I had little confidence that I would live long. But now I'm eighty-four [as of 2012] and still in good health. I feel that I have many years ahead of me yet.

Confidence is something you accumulate as you make your way through life. You can start by challenging some small, seemingly insignificant area of your life. For instance, if you continually oversleep, then getting up even five minutes earlier is a major accomplishment. That's human revolution. Please make that a source of confidence.

Challenge something. It doesn't matter what. It could be greeting people cheerfully, studying one more page in your textbook, or sticking to some after-school activity.

And if no one else applauds you, then congratulate yourself: "You did a good job!" "Your efforts paid off!"

Just remember, there are people who enjoy nothing more than finding fault with others. If you do something good and worthwhile, you'll be envied and resented. The world's values are upside down. So you need to be your own best friend and encourage yourself.

Of course, you can't hope to gain confidence if you expect others to do everything for you and don't put forth any real effort yourself. Self-confidence is built through exerting yourself. If you do your best in everything, you'll gain self-confidence. You'll be able to persevere and achieve anything you aim for. That, in turn, will bolster your self-confidence. It's a process of believing in yourself come what may, continuing to make efforts, and challenging yourself.

Society is filled with constant noise and chatter. People are consumed with trivial, superficial things. It's like when a light breeze blows and causes ripples on the water. There may be times when self-serving individuals seem to be the center of everyone's attention. But please don't allow your-self to be swayed by such shallow, transitory things.

Musashi closes with the message that we should lead our lives with confidence and strength, untroubled by the hubbub of the times. Whatever others may say, just forge ahead. Lead honorable lives with conviction as deep as the sea. That's the hallmark of genuine victors in life. It's also the way to form great friendships.

"Like Mount Fuji" has become a byword I share with many of my friends around the world. You, junior high and high school students, have faith in the Mystic Law. That is the most powerful conviction we can have. All of you are my direct disciples and successors. From today, please always advance with the serene dignity, confidence, and pride of Mount Fuji.

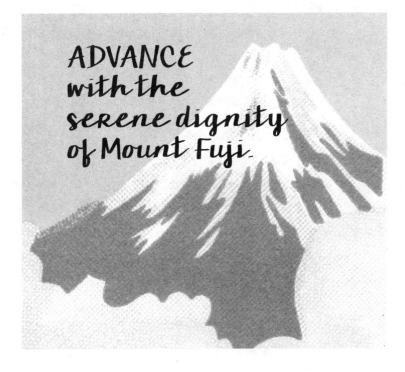

ADVANCE with the serene dignity of Mount Fuji.

Friendship Is a
TREASURE

Future Journal: *Members of the junior high and high school divisions in Japan and around the world are reading this series, and we have received many emails and letters saying that they feel like you are speaking directly to them.*

President Ikeda: Yes, I'd like to say: You, my young friends of the future division, are my life. I listen to what you're saying, and I understand your feelings. I know that you are bravely challenging all kinds of problems.

FJ: *We were surprised at the large number of readers who wrote in about problems they were having with their friends and asking for advice on how to solve them. Some common themes were difficulty communicating and interacting with classmates and not knowing how to make up with friends after a disagreement or quarrel.*

President Ikeda: The fact that you want to improve the situation shows that you are growing. It is because these things matter to you that you worry about them.

There are many great works of literature that have taken up the theme of friendship. The fact that stories of friendship like **Run, Melos!** by Osamu Dazai and **Jean-Christophe** by Romain Rolland, which were popular in my youth, are still widely read in Japan today shows that people care deeply about friendship.

Rather than letting worries about friendship consume you, I suggest you turn to the wisdom of great literature or famous people of the past. Use them as a reference and try to look at your problems calmly and with a broad mind.

FJ: *Some readers also said that while they have many friends, they don't have a best friend.*

President Ikeda: There is no need to be anxious about that. You are young, and this is just the beginning of your personal story of friendship.

In your teens, you begin to establish your own personality and way of looking at things. You may find yourself having less in common with friends that you used to get along with really well. Sometimes you may feel lonely. That's because all of you are growing and maturing. Day after day, your body, mind, and intellect are developing. The kind of friendships you want will also change and mature. This is all part of cultivating your independence and becoming an adult. By feeling loneliness and frustration along the way, you will learn who the really important people are in your lives.

When I was nineteen, just before I met Mr. Toda, I had many long, heart-to-heart talks with one of my good friends about life and philosophy. My friend decided to embrace the Christian faith. Though I didn't have an in-depth understanding of Christianity, I respected his decision, and we each began to follow our chosen paths. It was as I wrote in my poem "Morigasaki Beach":

Although different from the far-off world my friend seeks, I have my own way and path.[5]

I still consider him a dear friend and continue to chant for him.

After World War II, the values that had guided the Japanese people's lives until then all collapsed. I was seriously searching for the correct way to live. It was at that time that I encountered Josei Toda, who became my mentor in life. When I met him, I thought, "This is the person I have been looking for."

As Mr. Toda's disciple, having been trained and taught by him for many years, I went on to make friends with countless people around the world. I also share indestructible ties of friendship with all my fellow members in faith, grounded in the common wish for kosen-rufu.

FJ: *Readers also mentioned various other human relations problems they were having. Some said that they found themselves avoiding people they didn't like or snapping at their own friends or treating them coldly over something trivial. Some also asked how to interact with people they found hard to deal with.*

President Ikeda: We're all human, so it's only natural that we'll have our personal likes and dislikes.

Sometimes, precisely because you are good friends with someone, you will argue or disagree with them. You may also find that a person you thought you didn't like, whom you kept your distance from, is actually someone you can get along with very well.

Therefore, just be yourself and try to be pleasant and friendly. Slowly work on developing your character in a way that is true to yourself. Through trial and error, slowly gain the ability and wisdom to get along and work together with others.

I remember one evening when I was having a long, leisurely conversation with two dear friends, one from the United Kingdom and the other from China. At one point, we agreed that the **Analects** of Confucius was right when it said, "A gentleman gathers friends through his culture; and with these friends, he develops his humanity."[6] Friendship has two "wings" that allow us to soar to lofty heights, unswayed by our likes or dislikes. One is the desire to learn. The other is personal development. Good friends gather around those who strive to learn and improve themselves. And it is among good friends that we can polish our character. Friendship between people who aspire for lofty goals can multiply the fruits of their labor many times over.

> Good friends gather around those who strive to learn and improve themselves.

In particular, the friendships of your student days—as you study and grow together in a spirit of friendly rivalry—can be a wonderful source of inspiration. As you move beyond petty likes and dislikes and together try to improve yourselves, you will unlock your own potential. Not only that, but you will also bring out the good points in others. And you will be able to respect one another and applaud one another's strengths.

I would like all of you to experience the true richness of this kind of friendship.

FJ: *Some readers said that responding promptly to emails or text messages from school friends had become such an issue among teens recently that even a small delay could seriously sour friendships.*

President Ikeda: Cell phones are convenient, but they seem to make people very impatient, don't they!

Naturally, everyone appreciates a quick response. I personally have always believed in responding promptly with messages or words of thanks.

But it is certainly not wise, if, as students, you become obsessed with answering email and texts so that it interferes with your studies or sleep. I hope you'll handle this sensibly and not cause your parents to worry. Remember, a genuine, caring friend will understand if you are a little late getting back to them.

Among my friends around the world, there are many whom, because we each have such busy schedules, I have met in person only a few times. There are even some whom I've never met in person but only through letters.

Though I met Chinese premier Zhou Enlai only once, I am confident that our friendship is eternal. Why? Because I will always believe in him and share his spirit. Even though he is no longer here, our friendship will endure along with my own unchanging commitment.

FJ: *You have spoken many times about the novel **The Eternal City** by Hall Caine as an example of a story of undying friendship.*

President Ikeda: Yes, Mr. Toda actually gave me a copy of *The Eternal City*, saying, "This is for you." I fondly remember reading it and then lending it to other members to read as well.

The Eternal City tells the story of the youthful revolutionary David Rossi and his comrade in the struggle, Bruno. Set in Rome in 1900, it describes Rossi rising up to fight to establish a "Republic of Man." Rossi is persecuted by the dictator at the time, and Bruno is arrested and tortured.

While in jail, Bruno is shown a forged letter that says that Rossi has betrayed him. Nevertheless, he refuses to betray Rossi to the very end. He dies crying out, "Long live David Rossi!"[7] Another character in the novel praises Bruno's final words as "a voice of triumph . . . over self."[8]

A crown of victory shines in the hearts of those who believe in their friends to the very end.

The greatness of Rossi and Bruno's friendship lay in the strength of both their trust for each other and their commitment to their ideal of truth and justice. This unrivaled inner strength was forged through adversity. As Rossi says to Bruno, "That man is strongest who is strong through suffering."[9]

If you become strong, you can build golden friendships that nothing can ever destroy. Friendship always starts with you. To build an honorable friendship, you must uphold honorable ideals yourself and live out your youth in an honorable way. "Though others might betray me, I will never do the same to them!" Those who live with such integrity and commitment, who remain brave and faithful, are writing a brilliant drama of eternal victory.

I can confidently declare, based on my tireless struggles over the past six decades and more, that the essence of friendship is to be found in the care and support of our fellow members in faith.

In his treatise "On Establishing the Correct Teaching for the Peace of the Land," Nichiren Daishonin uses the expression "a friend in the orchid room" (WND-1, 23). Orchids in a room will impart their fragrance to all who enter. In the same way, good friends who gradually influence us through their presence or example are "friends in the orchid room." Building more of these kinds of friendships is the way to establish a society of peace and justice.

I place great faith in friendship. I'd like to share the words of the ancient Roman philosopher Cicero with you: "Friendship both enhances the splendour of good fortune, and by sharing and dividing troubles makes them easier to bear."[10]

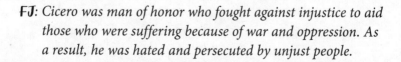

FJ: *Cicero was man of honor who fought against injustice to aid those who were suffering because of war and oppression. As a result, he was hated and persecuted by unjust people.*

President Ikeda: Yes. And it was true friends who encouraged and supported him during his trials. He could keep going because he had good friends.

It is more enjoyable to laugh with a friend than to laugh alone. A friend who rejoices with us in our successes doubles our joy. Having a friend who listens to your problems can be comforting. When you're facing something difficult or painful, having a friend say "Don't worry, it will be all right" can warm your heart and give you the strength to tackle the problem.

Friends are treasures. They are shining suns of hope, stars sparkling in the winter skies of adversity. They are a refreshing, comforting breeze, a bubbling spring that can revive our hearts.

Likewise, friendship is a great ship of courage for sailing together toward our dreams, a jet engine of wisdom for soaring together into the big, wide world.

"Beyond this ocean are vast continents. You must open the way of worldwide kosen-rufu in my stead."

—Josei Toda

DREAMS Are the Key to Unlock a Brilliant Future

Future Journal: The Soka Family Month is underway in Japan. With the support of their families, our young members are cheerfully engaging in various activities this summer.

President Ikeda: Summer is a time for youth to grow by leaps and bounds. I'm really looking forward to all of you growing wonderfully. I am chanting seriously that all of you will be healthy and safe, that you will have an enjoyable and meaningful summer.

When summer comes around, a vivid memory always returns to me. It is of the ocean off the coast of Atsuta in Hokkaido. My mentor, Mr. Toda, had taken me with him to visit Atsuta, his hometown, and we were gazing out at the sea together. I was twenty-six. Dyed crimson by the setting sun, the ocean off Atsuta stretched on forever. It was spectacular.

Mr. Toda firmly said to me: "Beyond this ocean are vast continents. The world is a big place, and many of its people are afflicted by terrible suffering. You must open the way of worldwide kosen-rufu in my stead."

Josei Toda

From that conversation, I made my mentor's dream of worldwide kosen-rufu my own. It is the dream of opening the way to happiness and peace for all, eradicating misery from the face of the earth, and enabling people to experience the true joy of living.

At that time [1954], the Soka Gakkai was still small. Worldwide kosen-rufu seemed like some fantasy. No one imagined it was possible. But I vowed deep in my heart that I would make that dream a reality, and that vow became my life.

FJ: *Once, when you were speaking to students at the Kansai Soka Junior High and High Schools, you replied to the question "What is your dream?" by saying, "My dream is making Mr. Toda's dream a reality."*

President Ikeda: Mr. Toda dedicated his life to a great dream—a dream shining with hope. He shared his dream with us, the youth, and showed us the correct way to move forward.

Even when his businesses were in crisis, he continued to talk about big dreams and goals. It was in fact then that he proposed founding a Soka Gakkai newspaper that people everywhere would read and establishing a university that would rank among the best in the world.

I went on to realize all of Mr. Toda's dreams. And as I did so, amazingly all of my own dreams from the time I was your age also came true. For example, I had always wished to plant cherry trees across Japan and to write an unforgettable novel.

And now I have a new dream: that your dreams will also come true. The dreams you imagine carry on my dreams. Each step you take toward realizing your dreams is a step toward realizing my dreams. I want us to share our dreams and achieve them together. Toward that end, I will continue to chant for you, watch over you, and support you. That is how I feel.

FJ: *Recently, it's been said that the present gloomy state of affairs in society makes it difficult for young people to feel hopeful or have dreams.*

President Ikeda: All young people have the right to dream whatever they want. It's not something that adults or the times can dictate. Precisely because these are such challenging times, I hope all of you will have bright dreams. I hope you share them widely and change the world.

Your dream can be anything, even if it's vague right now. It can be something small. Don't think about whether you can realize it or not. The first step is to envision it.

Once you've made up your mind, have the courage to take the first step. Once you do, the way forward will begin to reveal itself. Just keep pressing straight ahead. There will be times when you have second thoughts and times when you hit a wall. All these things show that you are growing. When you break through your current limitations, new horizons will open up before you. That is why it's important to keep challenging yourself, to keep on going no matter what.

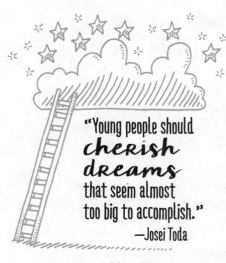

"Young people should *cherish dreams* that seem almost too big to accomplish."
—Josei Toda

Mr. Toda said: "Young people should cherish dreams that seem almost too big to accomplish." As future division members, you are practicing Nichiren Buddhism, which teaches us how to achieve absolute victory in life. No prayer based on faith in the Mystic Law goes unanswered.

Prayer is the source of victory. When serious prayer and hard work come together, dreams begin to come true.

FJ: *Talking about the ocean and dreams, I am reminded of one courageous Japanese youth who fulfilled his dream of becoming the first person to sail solo across the Pacific Ocean five decades ago [in 1962].*

President Ikeda: Yes, that was Kenichi Horie. I know him well. Since then, he has crossed the Pacific Ocean numerous times. He is one of my dear and respected friends.

Several years ago [from October 2004 to June 2005], Mr. Horie completed a nonstop solo circumnavigation of the globe. While he was at sea, I sent him messages from time to time, particularly when he was beginning difficult stretches, such as sailing around Cape Horn at the southern tip of South America.

This venerable adventurer expressed high hopes for SGI youth. He said: "I would like young people to turn their dreams into concrete goals and actively challenge themselves to realize them. . . . Nothing will change if we just think about doing something but take no action. . . . And if you try and fail, that's perfectly okay. Experiencing failure often turns out to be a truly valuable learning experience."[11]

No matter your dream, when you start to challenge yourself to realize it, the adventure begins.

I once asked Lester Thurow, a leading American economist, what true wealth meant for him. He replied without hesitation: a spirit of adventure and inquiry. Professor Thurow is himself an adventurer who has climbed twenty-three-thousand-foot peaks in the Himalayas and driven across the Saudi Arabian desert.

I completely agree that a spirit of adventure and inquiry, not money, constitutes true wealth. As long as this spirit is alive in young people's hearts, humanity can continue to pioneer new frontiers.

FJ: *There are still many mysteries in the world and the universe waiting to be solved. Just last month [on July 4, 2012], physicists announced the discovery of the Higgs boson, a particle for which they had long been searching.*

President Ikeda: Yes. In the world of science and learning, many people are on an adventure to pursue far-reaching dreams. Much remains to discover about the inner realm of the human being too. You are pioneers in this sphere. You have begun to explore in your youth the great philosophy of respect for the dignity of life that is Nichiren Buddhism.

Within each of you lies unimaginably wondrous power and potential. As you challenge yourself to realize your dreams, you'll come to discover that power and potential. There is no more thrilling adventure in life than this.

FJ: *Some future division members say that the gap between their dreams and reality is so huge that they feel powerless to bridge it.*

President Ikeda: They must have big dreams. How wonderful. There's bound to be some kind of gap between dreams and reality. Any dream that's easy to attain isn't very exciting. To realize our dreams, we need to have commitment and determination.

Thomas Edison was said to have been a poor student in school, but his drive to make life more convenient for everyone led him to become a great inventor. And for the

Wright brothers, their dream to fly like a bird helped them surmount a long series of failures and finally invent the first powered airplane. Though facing many obstacles, these great individuals held fast to their dreams and worked hard to make it a reality. They never gave up on it, even when others made fun of them or said it was impossible.

Indian champion of nonviolence Mahatma Gandhi; American civil rights leader Dr. Martin Luther King Jr.; and my dear friend Nelson Mandela, the former South African president who helped bring an end to apartheid—these three great individuals faced their struggles with unstoppable determination. Because of that, each could achieve a dream of freedom and equal rights that no one in the twentieth century believed could be realized.

Former Russian cosmonaut Valentina Tereshkova, with whom my wife and I enjoy a close friendship, bravely pursued her dream and became the first woman in space. Today, she continues to actively work for world peace.

I would like to share her words with you:

"We must fight for the sake of the future and courageously overcome every difficulty.

Valentina Tereshkova

That is the only way to achieve our aims and make even the boldest dreams come true."[12]

FJ: *Recent surveys have shown that Japanese teenagers today dream of having a secure and steady job. They listed occupations such as doctor, nurse, lawyer, civil servant, salaried corporate employee, and successor to their family business. Professional athlete and entertainer also ranked as popular choices.*

President Ikeda: These are all fine aspirations. Finding a job in your chosen field and working to be the absolute best is a wonderful thing. But I hope that you will think a little deeper. I hope you will ask yourself why, for what purpose, you are pursuing your particular dream.

Kosen-rufu is a dream that benefits not only ourselves but also others. It is a dream that we can all rejoice in, a dream of building a world of peace and happiness for everyone. Many of your mothers and fathers, and maybe even your grandmothers and grandfathers are striving alongside me for the sake of the highest ideal of kosen-rufu. They play their own unique part in the communities where they live and carry out their missions. In an age of self-centeredness, they concern themselves with the welfare of others and society and work tirelessly for that cause. No life is more admirable.

> Kosen-rufu is a dream of building a world of peace and *happiness for everyone*.

To some of you, it may seem that they put in more effort than it's worth. It may seem that what they're doing is time-consuming and unexciting. But from the perspective of Buddhism, their lives are supremely noble and honorable.

FJ: *How fortunate we are to work for such a lofty dream within the SGI.*

President Ikeda: I hope you, my young friends, will continue in your studies. I hope you will joyfully live each day with honor and pride, cherishing wonderful, exciting dreams as big as the universe.

Nichiren writes to his young disciple Nanjo Tokimitsu, "My wish is that all my disciples make a great vow" (WND-1, 1003). Here, to make a great vow means to dedicate our lives to the Mystic Law and the realization of kosen-rufu. Nichiren likens this to "a drop of dew rejoining the ocean, or a speck of dust returning to the earth" (WND-1, 1003). Our lives may seem fragile and fleeting like a drop of dew. But when we fuse them with the vast ocean of the universe, we can gain a boundless state of being. We may seem as small and insignificant as a speck of dust. But when we ground ourselves in the great earth of life, we can become an immense source of support for others and a wellspring of infinite creativity.

You who uphold the Mystic Law from such a young age are the hope and dream of humanity. If you dedicate your lives to the dream of bringing peace to our planet, the world will move closer to peace.

When we have a dream, we can grow without end.

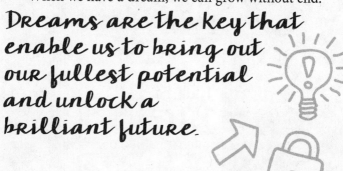

Dreams are the key that enable us to bring out our fullest potential and unlock a brilliant future.

Those Who Continue
LEARNING
Are Victors in Life

Future Journal: *The new semester has started in Japan [September 2012]. Also, those planning to take entrance examinations next year are studying hard.*

President Ikeda: I am praying wholeheartedly that everyone will advance along the path of hope, diligent effort, and victory. To those of you preparing for entrance examinations, please know that your fellow members are cheering you on.

Yeah!

Thinking back, it was in September 1945, when I was seventeen, that I began to attend night school. It was just a month after World War II ended. I remember facing the burned-out vista of Tokyo, razed by incendiary bombs, and being determined to learn. I told myself that now was the time to study for all I was worth.

I am still studying today. My dialogues with leading world figures are a continual process of learning and conversing, conversing and learning. Through this series, I also look forward to learning a great deal from you.

FJ: *Being able to study to our heart's content is in itself a great fortune, isn't it?*

President Ikeda: Yes. Learning is a right and a pleasure. Nothing is more enjoyable.

The brutal war, however, robbed young people my age of that right and joy. I was determined that the next generation should not be deprived of that, and I have fought all my life for peace.

That's why I would like to share with you these words of the German writer Goethe, whom I read avidly in my youth: **"What a world of delight lies in learning!"**[13] When you throw yourself into the world of learning, you'll make many new and exciting discoveries. It was this joy that pulsed in Goethe's life. A poet, novelist, playwright, naturalist, and political leader,

Johann Wolfgang von Goethe

Goethe continued learning throughout his life.

I am in a dialogue about Goethe with Dr. Manfred Osten of the Goethe Society in Weimar, Germany.[14] Dr. Osten has spoken of Goethe's conviction that no one can take away what you have learned through hard work—it is yours forever.

Human beings are born to learn. Life is an ongoing learning process. Even if we sometimes forget exactly what we have learned, the desire to learn forever adorns our lives.

FJ: *Some junior high and high school students say that though they want to do their best, they just don't feel motivated.*

President Ikeda: That's true for everyone! But wanting to do your best is in itself an admirable thing.

Even the world-renowned historian Arnold J. Toynbee told me that if he waited until he felt like doing his research, he'd never accomplish anything. He, therefore, made it a practice to sit down at his desk at a set time each day and start working, whether he felt like it or not.

If you get into the habit of studying, you will naturally feel more motivated. You'll find learning interesting and come to appreciate the importance of trying. I hope you'll all do your best to get into the habit of studying and don't give up until you do.

FJ: *It's important for us to ask ourselves why we're studying, isn't it?*

You gave Soka University the motto "For what purpose should one cultivate wisdom? May you always ask yourself this question!"

President Ikeda: I hope you will continue to ask yourselves the purpose of your learning as long as you live.

If you're studying only for yourself, eventually you will

hit a dead end. But when you have a larger purpose—such as studying for the sake of others, for society, and for the world—studying becomes fun. And in the process, you'll build yourself into a great human being too.

In 1995, I visited Nepal, where Shakyamuni Buddha was born. After speaking at Tribhuvan University, I attended an SGI-Nepal general meeting. I was welcomed there by five young girls dressed in scarlet native costumes and wearing gold ornaments in their hair.

Five girls in native costumes welcome the SGI president after an SGI-Nepal general meeting.

Later, with their parents' warm encouragement, these young girls went on to apply themselves to their studies. They were determined to become capable people themselves so that they could help foster many others. They hoped to become leaders who could play a positive role in society for the happiness and welfare of the people. Though they experienced setbacks along the way, they persevered. They kept going because they believed in themselves and knew that their parents were behind them 100 percent. Today, seventeen years later [in 2012], they are succeeding in their studies and are contributing to society. They are a great source of pride and inspiration to their parents and fellow members in Nepal. Many future division members are following in their footsteps.

The more you study, the greater your dreams expand. You become more capable and accomplished and can help others. You can bring smiles to people's faces and impart joy. You end up creating a wonderful environment around you.

FJ: *Sometimes adults regret not having studied harder in high school.*

President Ikeda: There's no need to look back with regrets. You can start studying from the place in life you are at this moment.

When she was sixty, the German author Malwida von Meysenbug declared: "I study and study. . . . For the sole reason of being able to study more would I wish to be young again!"[15]

Academic credentials are not the same as what you really know or your ability to learn, and it is even less a measure of the full scope of a person's potential. A person's true capability can be measured by their desire to continue learning.

In April [2012], two women aged eighty-three and eighty-five graduated from the Soka University's Division of Correspondence Education. Those who study in earnest shine with a noble and inspiring light.

FJ: *When we're young and have the perfect opportunity to study, though, we tend to put off studying.*

President Ikeda: Well, we can all come up with plenty of reasons for procrastinating, can't we? It may be that we find the subject too difficult to understand. Or just as we were about to sit down at our desk, our father or mother tells us to study, and that makes us even less inclined to do so! Or we have sports practice or other extra-curricular activities to attend.

But what if it's a subject we really like? In that case, I think many of us can get started right away and keep at it for hours, totally engrossed.

If you wanted to learn how to become better at soccer or how to play an instrument like a favorite musician or know what kind of clothes were going to be in fashion in the fall—then, I'm sure, you would read any number of books, try out certain techniques, and ask questions. You'd find it fun and interesting. You need to find ways to motivate yourself in your studies in the same way, so that they become just as enjoyable and absorbing.

FJ: *Successful people in any field invariably study very hard.*

President Ikeda: True. Top athletes don't train only their bodies. Many of them also study about how the body works and about nutrition and other related fields. I know many actors and entertainers who read a huge number of books to polish their skills and help them play their roles.

Your parents, too, when it comes to knowing when and where to shop for groceries, have an expertise on a par with world-class economists! They constantly keep up on real-life economic trends.

These are all great examples of how valuable study can be.

I hope you'll look at your studies as laying the foundation for being able to study whatever you like in the future. You'd be amazed at how things that don't seem relevant now turn out to be incredibly useful later. Just try to make a start in something. Begin by making a small effort.

Being good or bad at studying is really just a matter of whether you try. You may find your studies now very boring, but in the process you will break out of the shell of your small self into the freedom of a much broader, greater realm. Your life will be illuminated. Learning is light.

Those who keep at their studies with a positive attitude, no matter what, are the ones who win out in the end.

FJ: *Many students ask how the things they have to study could possibly have any relevance to their futures.*

President Ikeda: When a building is under construction, the foundation doesn't give us any idea of what the finished structure will look like. And when the building is done, the foundation can no longer be seen. Yet it is that foundation that keeps the building standing for decades or even centuries.

The same is true of study. Each effort to challenge yourself builds your foundation.

Accepting the challenge to study is in itself a wonderful form of character building. It teaches you to think, trains your mind, and fosters inner strength. You are all building your foundations right now. It's hard, repetitive work. As a result, it may be boring. But hard, repetitive work is what makes a foundation indestructible. That's why it's important for you to do a little every day, the best you can, adding even just another millimeter or two to your foundation.

FJ: *Some say that they feel discouraged that they can't improve their grades.*

President Ikeda: Of course, it makes you and your parents happy when you improve your grades, and there's nothing better than that. But grades are not a true measure of your worth as a person. Don't compare yourself to others, and don't allow your grades to make you lose self-confidence.

Instead, you can make it a goal to improve your grades. You can try to raise them a little at a time. I hope you will challenge yourselves like this. Even if you don't get the results you'd hoped for, the efforts you are making are surely helping you grow and develop. Over the long term, your grades are much less important than getting in the habit of learning and improving yourself. A person who is always ready and eager to learn creates a life of infinite possibilities.

It is never too late to begin studying seriously. Even if you have the lowest grades in the class now, you can still get better as long as you don't give up on yourself. And when you do improve, it will mean even more to you, because of where you started. The worst thing is to let failure make you stop studying.

Success is a matter of sticking to it. It's important to try your hardest. You can't expect results in a day. Keeping at it is what matters. Regard your studies as training to hone your mind and develop grit!

FJ: *During your youth, you received personal instruction from Mr. Toda.*

President Ikeda: Yes, and it was very demanding! My lessons with Mr. Toda were held when his businesses were in dire financial straits. It was a challenging period.

I wrote in my diary at the time: "The morning lecture has progressed from law, to politics, to economics, to science, to Chinese literature. How can I ever repay my debt of gratitude to my mentor, who has striven to raise this disciple without regard even for his own health? Now is the time to accumulate my power and ability. Must develop my capability in preparation for the time to come."[16]

Mr. Toda was well versed in many subjects. Moreover, he always taught in a way that what I was learning would have practical relevance. I also never knew when he might suddenly inquire, "What are you reading now?" and ask me to tell him what it was about. He always wanted to know what I thought of and what I'd learned from the books I'd read. Sometimes I'd break out into a cold sweat as I struggled to explain my thoughts coherently.

When one of his courses ended, he gave me a flower from a vase on his desk and placed it in my buttonhole. "This is your award for completing this course with top honors," he said. "I wish I could give you a gold watch or something, but unfortunately I don'thave anything."

That single flower I received from my mentor was, to me, the highest honor in the world. I am filled with gratitude, knowing that it was his instruction that has enabled me to carry on meaningful dialogues with many noted leaders from around the globe.

The victory of Soka mentors and disciples is the victory of continuous learning. That's why I pray earnestly every day that you, my young friends, will grow up to be outstanding leaders of sparkling intellect and goodness. I hope that you will make full use of your talents in whatever field you choose. It is also my wish that all of you lead victorious lives and that you and your families enjoy good health and boundless good fortune.

Please study hard in the new semester!

6

Keep Persevering With a Positive, Tenacious ATTITUDE

- - - - →

Future Journal: *We have been receiving many emails and letters from students around the world sharing how they are challenging themselves in various areas, including sports and other extracurricular activities.*

President Ikeda: That's wonderful! I also regularly receive many letters from future division members and leaders reporting on their activities and development. I also notice that our newspapers carry many articles on the outstanding achievements of future division members in sports, music, art, foreign language, and so on.

    The sight of our future division members challenging themselves and achieving successes must be a source of pride for their parents and families. It is also surely encourages and inspires the members of their local Soka families.

    Stories of success lift everyone's spirits. They spread hope and encourage others to challenge and polish themselves as well. But the road to self-improvement never ends. There is always room to learn more, to grow more. I hope you will keep pressing forward, always aspiring to reach new heights as you continue to develop your potential.

FJ: *Some students have shared being frustrated and disappointed when their best efforts failed to produce the outcome they'd hoped for.*

President Ikeda: In many competitive fields, victory often depends on luck. So there's no need to be obsessed with the outcome. If you've done your very best, then you have won.

By experiencing both victories and defeats, we grow stronger and more resilient. So please don't let a defeat or failure discourage you. What matters is that you remain unbeaten in spirit.

True victors are those who keep on smiling regardless of whether they win or lose and move on to the next challenge with even stronger determination.

FJ: *Some express frustration at not becoming as good as they'd like to be in their club activity or not being selected to play on their sports team.*

If you've done your very best, then you have won.

President Ikeda: It's quite natural, of course, that when you start out in something you won't become good at it overnight. Whatever the field, you have to begin with the basics and then work on getting better. The only way to become good at anything is to start at the beginning: learn the basics one by one from your teachers or coaches and from your teammates and fellow students. Then practice again and again. It's challenging and demanding. At times, it can also be repetitive, monotonous, and time-consuming. That's why it's important to remember why you wanted to do it in the first place and keep working steadily to hone your skills. If you're even a little better today than you were yesterday, that's an achievement. Your true rival is yourself—yesterday's self.

There will be times when it seems you are trying your hardest but not getting anywhere. That's when you need to just keep going. In fact, the times when you are struggling and challenging yourself the most are often the times when you can develop the greatest strength. Such training will not only help you in becoming a good athlete or doing well in your extracurricular activities, but it will also become a treasure for your entire life.

Even if you remain only a substitute player, that doesn't mean your practice and training were wasted. I know many people whose efforts out of the limelight when they were young helped shape them into individuals who are now playing important roles in society.

FJ: *Often, when we don't see any improvement despite all our efforts, we compare ourselves with others and get down on ourselves.*

President Ikeda: Don't let such a self-defeating attitude take over your life. Encourage yourself. Keep trying. Stay positive and be persistent so that you can come out ahead.

What is true talent? The German archaeologist Heinrich Schliemann said, "Talent means energy and persistence and nothing more."[17] He is absolutely right. Anyone can develop talent.

FJ: *Schliemann discovered the ruins of the ancient city of Troy, in 1870 realizing a lifelong dream. He also once visited Hachioji, Tokyo, where Soka University is.*[18]

President Ikeda: That's right. According to his autobiography, when he was eight, his father gave him a book with an illustration of the Trojan War. Looking at the picture, he pledged that he would someday find the city of Troy. Thus began a long and difficult struggle.

His mother died when he was still a boy, and then his father lost his job. The young Schliemann, therefore, had to start working instead of attending high school. He tried to study on his own, but by the time he had finished work, he was too exhausted to retain much of what he read. He knew, however, that he had to master foreign languages to achieve his dream. By means of a unique method of study that he devised himself, he became fluent in English, Greek, and another dozen or so languages.

He also worked very hard in the business world and amassed a large fortune, which he later used to fund his archaeological work. He was over forty before he could go on his first expedition in search of Troy.

Eventually he succeeded in finding the ancient city and proving the existence of Trojan and Mycenaean civilizations, which until that time had been regarded as purely

The Trojan Horse, ancient Troy

mythical. His success in realizing his dream is truly an expression of his belief that *"talent means energy and persistence."*

FJ: *To fulfill his dream, Schliemann patiently did what needed to be done, such as learning languages and earning a livelihood.*

President Ikeda: That's why he succeeded. If you apply yourself to what you *need* to do, you can definitely turn it into an asset for helping you accomplish what you *want* to do.

As students, study is your top priority, so right now it's the thing that you *need* to do. You may sometimes feel too tired from sports or other activities to open your books. But studying hard now will be to your benefit and help you realize your big dreams. I hope you'll develop a wise balance and put the determination and persistence you've cultivated through sports or other extracurricular activities to good use in your studies.

FJ: *Actually, many have asked how to find a balance between their studies and their extracurricular activities.*

President Ikeda: It certainly is a challenge. I spoke with a student who wondered whether it was wise for her to be involved in several extracurricular activities. I said: "There's an old saying, 'If you chase two hares, you will catch neither.' But, I say, if you have the energy, go ahead and chase a hundred or a thousand hares!" That gave her more confidence.

All of you are young, so I hope you'll have this kind of limitless ambition and freely cultivate your potential.

Instead of worrying about whether you can do something, just go ahead and try. Resolve to do your best in both your studies and your extracurricular activities. Then chant Nam-myoho-renge-kyo, bring forth your wisdom and resourcefulness, and challenge yourself. Through diligent trial and error, you'll find a way forward.

Dr. Vincent Harding is an American historian and human rights activist with whom I have published a dialogue. "When we think about athletes engaged in serious physical training," he said, "they develop capabilities . . . that they never imagined that they had. But sometimes," he continued, "we assume that we are limited. Through this mistaken assumption, we impose limits on the development of our potential."[19]

All of you have a potential that is as boundless as the universe itself. In addition, you have the good fortune of being able to embrace the Mystic Law at a young age.

Mr. Toda often used to say to us youth: "First, make a firm determination. And when you've done that, set out courageously."[20] Throw yourself 100 percent into the tasks at hand. Giving 100 percent to everything you do is the key to winning in youth.

> Giving 100 percent to everything you do is the key to *winning in youth.*

Naturally, when you have an exam coming up, you need to concentrate on studying. When you have a game coming up, you need to put aside time for training and practice. Setting priorities wisely in this way is also important.

FJ: *Some students are so busy with extracurricular activities that they don't have time to participate in SGI activities.*

President Ikeda: Buddhism teaches that what matters is our heart. Therefore, even if you can't always attend SGI meetings, wishing you could is itself admirable. It means your life is still moving in a positive direction, in the direction of solid growth.

Also, even if you can't make it to meetings, I hope you'll

keep your leaders and fellow members up to date on what you're doing and what your goals are. In the realm of the SGI, we are all linked together by our hearts and by our prayers.

Your fellow members are like supporters cheering you on and chanting for your growth. Your achievements become a source of joy for everyone. This in turn flows back to you as encouragement. You'll find that, at crucial moments, your fellow members will always be there for you.

Even if you don't have time to go to meetings very often, you can still stay connected with your fellow members in your heart. When you do have the time to attend, I hope you will go without the slightest hesitation. And remember, even though you may not always feel like going to a meeting, you'll invariably find yourself energized and inspired afterward if you do go.

FJ: *Many members have shared about the struggles they are having in their relationships. Some, for example, want to know how they can get along with their peers and what they should do when the atmosphere on their team or in their after-school club isn't good.*

President Ikeda: Such groups are a microcosm of society. Consequently, there will be people who share your goals and who can help you improve yourself. But there will also be others with whom you'll find it hard to get along. You may also have to deal with rivalry and sometimes even envy.

More than fifty years ago, I visited the ruins of Aoba Castle in Sendai, Miyagi Prefecture, with Mr. Toda. Looking at the imposing stone walls of the castle's foundation, he said, "The Gakkai will build its castle from capable people!"

The walls of Aoba Castle have stood for almost four hundred years.

Each stone in a castle wall is unique; not a single one is the same. They are all different shapes and sizes. But meticulous placement makes use of their individual characteristics, and they can form a wall that will stand for centuries.

The same is true of a team or club. By making the best use of the unique characteristics of the members, you can display even stronger teamwork than you imagined possible. It is in such a team or group that each individual's abilities come to shine. The way to create superb teamwork is to respect your teammates or colleagues. If you trust and respect one another, unity will happen naturally.

I hope all of you, as practitioners of the great teaching of Nichiren Buddhism, will become a sunny presence who can encourage others and see their strong points. If the mood in your team or club lacks spirit, be the sunshine that brightens and energizes everyone around you.

FJ: *Future division leaders ask what they need to do to get members to unite toward a goal. They also want to know how they should act as leaders.*

President Ikeda: Those are wonderful questions. Anyone thinking about such things is already a fine leader.

There are leaders who strive in the vanguard, who spearhead the way forward. Others support everyone from behind the scenes. Just be yourself, with your natural youthful energy. It's all a learning process.

Many of the great leaders of history, as well as the first-rate individuals with whom I've had dialogues, share one thing in common—passion. Passionate people inspire trust.

Passionate
people
inspire
trust.

If you really want to succeed, to grow along with everyone else, to unite your group, and to bring joy to everyone, you'll find the wisdom to achieve those things. Chanting for those goals will reach everyone else.

Mr. Toda offered me many lessons in leadership. He taught me the importance of being self-confident, sincere, and considerate, and of developing one's abilities. All of these things are supported and sustained by passion, conviction, and chanting Nam-myoho-renge-kyo.

Those who struggle and work hard can achieve great things. I hope that all of you, my dear members of the junior high and high school division, will persist in your efforts to grow and develop together with good friends. I am eagerly looking forward to the day when you play an active role on the world stage as outstanding leaders.

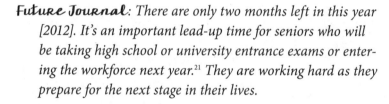

PROUDLY
Walk the Path of Self-Improvement

Future Journal: *There are only two months left in this year [2012]. It's an important lead-up time for seniors who will be taking high school or university entrance exams or entering the workforce next year.[21] They are working hard as they prepare for the next stage in their lives.*

President Ikeda: You, our future division members, are all immensely capable individuals. You will become the mainstays of society and the future leaders of the SGI. The entire Soka family is looking forward to your wonderful endeavors.

Those of you preparing for entrance exams need to take special care to stay well and not catch colds. I am chanting earnestly every day for your health and success.

FJ: *Many students say they don't know what they should do after graduation. They all seem to share a vague anxiety about the future. We often hear them saying that they have*

no idea what school to go to next or that they don't know
what direction to pursue because they have no clear dreams.

President Ikeda: I completely understand. Life is a series
of difficult choices. Entrance exams, in particular, probably
represent your first major turning point. It's only natural to
feel uncertain and anxious.

Don't keep your worries to yourself, however. Please
talk frankly with your parents, teachers, or other older
people whom you trust. Dare to dream big and choose the
best path.

I hope that you will press forward on your chosen
course without fear. The courage to
take the first step is what counts.

There are paths in the
sky that birds follow
and paths in the sea
that fish follow. The
sun steadily follows
its set course, whether
it's cloudy or raining.
Human beings, too,
have their path—one
seeking happiness and
self-improvement. It is a
path that enables us to keep
on developing ourselves and
growing wiser and stronger, no
matter what obstacles we may face.

EVERYONE HAS ONE'S OWN PATH

FJ: *Next year [2013], a new Arts and Sciences Building will open at Soka University, Japan. Many future division members are working hard to gain entrance to the Soka schools, including the Soka junior high and high schools in Tokyo and Osaka, Soka University, Soka Women's College, and Soka University of America.*

President Ikeda: As the founder, I am deeply gratified by this. If it were possible, I would admit everyone who applies, but unfortunately that can't be. Nevertheless, I still regard all applicants, accepted or not, as students of the Soka schools. I continue to pray that they all become happy and successful. I will never forget any of them. That is my spirit as the schools' founder.

Of course, you should feel free to apply to any school you want. Whatever you decide, I will support you with all my heart so that you may develop your full potential and enjoy success in whatever you choose.

FJ: *Whatever path a young person might choose, the important thing is that they keep on developing and improving themselves, isn't it?*

President Ikeda: Yes. The father of Soka education and the first Soka Gakkai president, Tsunesaburo Makiguchi, is an example of such a person. Mr. Makiguchi had to work

Tsunesaburo Makiguchi

from the time he was the age of many of you. But he used every spare moment he could find to study and learn. He eventually became an innovative geographer and a great educator.

Even after he was imprisoned for his struggle against Japanese militarism, until his death in prison, he continued to study and develop himself. This incomparably noble seeker of truth and wisdom is the founder of the Soka Gakkai.

I'd like to share with you some words of the Austrian poet Rainer Maria Rilke, a contemporary of Mr. Makiguchi. "Life is in the right, always,"[22] she writes, and "Everything that makes *more* of you than you have ever been, even in your best hours, is right."[23] These words may be a little difficult to understand, but they contain a profound message. The poet is urging us to push beyond our current best.

The path of personal growth is the correct path through life.

The path of personal growth is the *correct path through life.*

Things may not go exactly as you hope in your entrance exams or job hunting. Even so, if you resolve to take everything as an opportunity to grow, you will be on the right track and will ultimately win in life. As long as you have the spirit to keep on developing, you will never be on the wrong track. For that reason, there is nothing to fear.

In his youth, Rilke suffered because he couldn't decide his own path in life. His father, a former military officer, enrolled him in a military academy. Rilke hated it. He was bullied by other students, and eventually he dropped out. He next went to business school but had to withdraw from that too. It must have been difficult for him, and his father must have also been disappointed.

But Rilke resumed his studies and entered university. Soon after, he decided to devote himself to his true passion, writing. He went on to produce numerous poems and essays. Rilke came to view this period of his life as a time of self-examination, when he questioned whether he could really succeed on his chosen path.

He later met noted figures such as the Russian writer Leo Tolstoy and the French sculptor Auguste Rodin. These encounters inspired him to persist in his efforts. He carried on his creative struggle in a way that was true to himself, never letting his problems or troubles defeat him.

FJ: *It was that youthful struggle that enabled him to write poetry that still resonates powerfully with young people around the world today.*

President Ikeda: The spirit of youth is indomitable. Though you may stumble and fall, the important thing is to pull yourself up again. Don't let it get you down. Nichiren Buddhism teaches that our problems are the springboard for attaining enlightenment. If you base yourselves on your Buddhist practice, all of the problems you face will become treasures of the heart.

There's no need to worry even if right now you don't know what you want to do in the future. We are bombarded by all kinds of information. You may sometimes be swayed by pessimistic news reports or others' gloomy outlooks. So you may feel lost and discouraged when trying to figure out your future. There may also be times when you feel depressed when you compare grades with your friends. This is even more likely during the entrance exam period.

But, just as in the case of Rilke, throw yourself into tackling the things you need to do right now. Then you're certain to find your own path, one you can walk along with hope.

FJ: *As entrance exams approach, many students get anxious about certain subjects. Or they lose their confidence because they can't improve their grades.*

President Ikeda: The important thing is not to give up. By facing crucial challenges head-on and giving them your best shot, you will gain self-confidence. This will be a source of strength throughout your life.

Professor Toynbee told me that he had been incredibly worried about passing the entrance exam for a prestigious public school. His parents told him to just do his best and that the world wouldn't end if he didn't get into that school. Their advice reassured him, and he was able to do well.

A true victor is someone who can say, "I did the very best I could do."

Nichiren Daishonin writes, "Those who believe in the Lotus Sutra [Nam-myoho-renge-kyo] are as if in winter, but winter always turns to spring" (WND-1, 536).

It is because trees weather the harsh cold of winter that they bring forth beautiful, fragrant blossoms in the spring. No matter how cold it gets, trees endure patiently. They slowly but surely take in the nutrients they need. In every area of life, **challenges and crises make us stronger.**

We are now entering the cold winter months here in Japan. Let's support all our future division members who are taking entrance exams, so that they can continue with courage and usher in a spring of triumph. My foremost wish is that each future division member will grow into a fine adult. I hope all future division leaders will continue to watch over our young members and do your utmost to encourage and support them.

FJ: *Yes, we'll do our best to support them in every way possible.*

Some students also say that they would like to attend university, but their family situation makes it impossible. In these hard financial times, there are many cases in which parents simply can't afford to send their children to college.

President Ikeda: I am fully aware of how difficult it can be, and I am chanting seriously that such families will overcome their hardships through their Buddhist practice. No matter how tough their finances are, though, I would like to ask these members not to become negative or self-pitying.

Strong people are not forged in easy circumstances. I hope that, through your challenges, you will proudly and cheerfully forge an inner strength that shines like a diamond.

Mr. Toda graduated at the head of his class in higher elementary school [like today's junior high school]. But he couldn't go to secondary school because he had to help out with the family business. He didn't become disheartened, though. He later also worked at a small wholesale store, but he kept his love for learning alive. While working, he continued to study on his own and later became an elementary school teacher.

One of my dear friends, Dr. Cho Moon Boo, a former president of Jeju National University in South Korea, also had to give up his dream of going to high school. That's why, after struggling to complete his education and becoming a teacher himself, he often used his own salary to support young students. His painful setbacks and disappointments spurred him on in his pursuit of learning and forged his character.

How we lead our lives is up to us. It is not determined by our environment. We create our environment. We open the way for ourselves. The purpose of faith is to keep that spirit alive in our hearts.

WE OPEN THE WAY FOR OURSELVES. THE PURPOSE OF FAITH IS TO KEEP THAT *spirit alive in our hearts.*

FJ: *I once heard a Soka University student speak of his experience of being bullied in elementary school and junior high. After hearing one of your speeches, he made a fresh determination and overcame his situation. He later began studying seriously so that he could apply for Soka University. But his father passed away and the family finances became tight. He thought he might have to abandon his dream. Nevertheless, he continued chanting to attend because he was deeply grateful for your guidance that had been such a lifeline to him. Then, unexpectedly, someone offered to assist him with tuition. He was also able to avail himself of Soka University's financial assistance and scholarship program.*

He is now a doctorate student at Soka University, studying hard and supporting his juniors.

President Ikeda: That's wonderful. He made the impossible possible.

Learning is light. The path of learning is bright. If you want to learn, you will find a way. That is why it's important to never lose the desire to learn and grow. Please keep forging ahead. The path you are on will become the path on which you fulfill your mission and find victory. You have that power. You have that potential.

Let's continue moving forward, ever forward, chanting Nam-myoho-renge-kyo—the key to tapping the boundless power within us—as we

proudly walk the path of self-improvement.

8

Having Appreciation for One's PARENTS

President Ikeda: I sincerely commend each of you, my young friends in the future division, for the earnest efforts you have made this year. Please be extra careful to avoid accidents in this busy year-end period [December 2012]. I am chanting every day for your health, safety, and victory—especially for those of you who are preparing for high school or university entrance exams.

In Japan, December is traditionally known as *Shiwasu* [written with the Chinese characters meaning "mentor" or "teacher" and "to run"].[24] Mr. Toda once said with a smile: "Just as the literal meaning of *Shiwasu* indicates, 'teachers are running' too. I know you are busy, but I am also running at full speed! Please all do your best for kosen-rufu as well."

Many of your parents are working hard to bring happiness to their communities and peace to the world as SGI members. They are supremely noble "emissaries of the Buddha" and "treasures of the nation." I am filled with infinite gratitude for them.

I hope you will all care for your wonderful parents and be good sons and daughters to them.

Future Journal: You always stress the importance of appreciating one's parents. As a result, many future division members have said that they plan to do something nice for their parents during the upcoming New Year's holiday, such as helping them out around the house and so on.

President Ikeda: I'm sure your parents will be touched by such thoughtful gestures. You'll not only help relieve your parents' stress, but you might even get a larger New Year's gift! [In Japan, it is a tradition at the new year for parents or visitors to give children a small gift of money.]

I once wrote a poem for high school students:

> **Excellence**
> **and appreciation for one's parents**
> **go hand in hand.**

Having appreciation for one's parents is the art of humanity, the ultimate path to happiness, and the foundation for world peace.

FJ: Some students have written that they would like to be good to their parents and show their appreciation, but they don't know how to go about it.

President Ikeda: Buddhism teaches three ways of being a good son or daughter. The first is to give them clothing, food, or some such daily necessities. The second is to respond to their wishes. While both of these may be important, the third and highest form is to help direct your parents' lives toward eternal happiness through the power of faith in the Mystic Law.

In other words, the best way to be good sons and daughters is to chant Nam-myoho-renge-kyo, the Law of the universe, and become outstanding individuals based on practicing Nichiren Buddhism.

For now, being good sons and daughters means studying your hardest and developing yourselves so that one day you can lead many others to happiness and contribute to society and the world. For parents, there is surely no greater pride or joy than to have their child grow into a person whom others look up to and appreciate. It makes them feel that all their efforts to raise their child have been rewarded.

The best way for you to be good sons and daughters is through your own growth and victory. The parent-child relationship continues no matter your age. A parent is always a parent, and a child always a child. Even after death, the lives of parent and child remain connected. From that perspective, being good sons and daughters takes a lifetime. The key is to steadily polish and develop yourselves, without being impatient.

With this in mind, I'd like to share with you some words of José Rizal, the renowned champion of Philippine independence: "The greatest honor that [one] can pay to [one's] parents is honesty and a good name."[25]

José Rizal

FJ: *Rizal died at the young age of thirty-five, giving his life to the struggle to free his homeland from colonial oppression. He was a true Renaissance man—a linguist, poet, novelist, physician, artist, agronomist, and educator.*

President Ikeda: That's right. His diverse talent resulted from the attentive education he received from his parents, particularly his mother. From the time he was a boy, his mother encouraged him to read and also often read to him. The stories she told him sustained him throughout his life. He also studied languages with his mother and cultivated a spirit of global citizenship, eventually mastering twenty-two languages.

At one point, Rizal's mother was imprisoned for two and a half years on false charges. A learned woman, she refused to submit to the unjust demands of the colonial authorities. This defiance angered them. Witnessing the terrible injustice committed by those in power, Rizal vowed to work to free his homeland. He stood up for his mother and for his country. His courageous spirit still shines undimmed in the Philippines today.

FJ: *Rizal's determination to repay his gratitude to his parents helped him remain strong in the face of persecution.*

President Ikeda: Yes. A favorite Okinawan folk song of

mine, "Balsam Flowers," has the lyrics: **"Though we might count the stars in the heavens, / we cannot count the lessons of our parents."**

Your parents work very hard to bring you up, though you may not see it. When you realize how much you owe them and resolve to repay them in some way, you will be filled with great energy and strength. When Nichiren was twelve, he vowed to repay his gratitude to his parents by becoming the "wisest person in all Japan" (WND-1, 175).

Our heart, our intent, is indeed the foundation for everything. If you have even the wish to show your appreciation to your parents, there is no limit to the growth you can achieve. The next step, of course, is showing that appreciation in some concrete way. Addressing his youthful disciple Nanjo Tokimitsu, the Daishonin recommends that when you want to give your parents something nice but don't have anything on hand, just give them a smile two or three times a day (see WND-2, 636). This is clear and simple advice.

As future division members, you have yet to enter the workforce, so buying expensive gifts for your parents will only cause them to worry. But smiles don't cost anything. You can withdraw limitless smiles from the bank of your heart. It is a gift that will please your parents most. A smiling child is a source of unconditional happiness for a loving parent.

FJ: *Some say they feel too embarrassed or awkward to give their parents a smile.*

President Ikeda: That's all part of being the age you are right now. To a certain extent, it can't be helped. But if you find it difficult to smile, at least try to speak in a pleasant tone. Responding nicely when your parents ask you something is important. That's the trick for reassuring them. For example, when your parents wish you a good day as they see you off to school, respond with a cheerful, "See you later!" When they ask if you're doing your homework, just say, "Yes, I'm doing it now!" And when they tell you to turn the TV off, call out, "Okay, I will in a minute!" Whatever the situation, responding in an upbeat way will put your parents' minds at ease.

But if you respond to "Did you do your homework?" "It's time to go to bed," and "Did you brush your teeth?" with an irritated, "Get off my back!" "I don't want to!" or "Leave me alone!" your parents will feel bad and unappreciated. The fact is, it's the job of parents to be on your back. You'll be better off if you just say to yourself, "Well, I'm glad they have the energy to keep after me the way they do."

You'd be surprised how trying to respond positively can lift both your own spirits and those of your parents. It will make your family a warmer, happier place. That's the power your words can have.

Words Have POWER!

FJ: *Emphasizing the power of our voice and words, the Daishonin says, "The voice carries out the work of the Buddha" (OTT, 4).*

President Ikeda: The Mongolian poet Gombojavyn Mend-Ooyo recently visited the Soka Junior High and High Schools in Tokyo [November 17, 2012]. He once said: "Nothing is more powerful than words. Depending on how they are used, they can function as 'words of light' that brighten people's hearts."

The important thing is to try to express your sincere feelings. Tell them, "I really appreciate you," "I chant for your good health every day," or "I promise to make you proud and take you on an overseas trip one day!" Just say those kinds of things from time to time. Your parents might be startled and ask if you're running a fever, but they will actually be delighted.

The point is that being good to your parents doesn't have to involve doing anything special. Just getting up on time every morning, eating your breakfast, and going to school; studying hard; staying on good terms with your friends—all of those can be ways of being good sons and daughters. They will reassure your parents and keep them from worrying about you.

FJ: *There are also some future division members who feel sad because they don't have a mother or a father.*

President Ikeda: I know how those of you who are in this situation must feel. But you are all young lions. I hope you will be strong, bright, and live proudly. If you don't have a father, then be twice as good to your mother. Likewise, if you don't have a mother, be doubly supportive of your father.

For those of you who have experienced the death of a parent, please know that they remain alive in your heart. When you chant to the Gohonzon, you can find them there. You are connected through your chanting. Your deceased mother or father is always watching over your growth. They are applauding your efforts, without a doubt.

In a letter to a follower who had lost both parents, the Daishonin writes that [your] head is the head of [your] parents, [your] feet are their feet, [your] ten fingers are their ten fingers, [your] mouth is their mouth (see WND-2, 658).

This means that all the benefit you gain through your efforts for kosen-rufu, using the body you received from your parents, will flow on to the lives of your parents as well.

When you are victorious, your parents are victorious.

FJ: *Some say that no matter how hard they try, they cannot respect their parents.*

President Ikeda: That's all right for now. Remember, you are who you are, aside from your parents. Just strive to become the best person you can. This is your precious youth.

If you have tough problems at home that you can't deal with on your own, please find a trusted senior in faith you can talk to. But don't forget that you should greatly appreciate your parents simply for giving you the gift of life. Parents are people too. They aren't perfect. I hope you will try to be mature enough to imagine their problems and the things they are going through.

Mr. Toda was well aware that some young people had difficulties with their parents. Yet he still made the strict point that those who can't have compassion for their parents cannot carry out kosen-rufu. The bonds of parent and child are mysterious and have unfathomably deep meaning. From the profound point of view of Buddhism, we have chosen to be born to our parents so that we may fulfill our great mission in this lifetime. Therefore, appreciating our parents expresses our gratitude for being born and being alive. The wish to repay the gratitude we owe our parents enables us to open up and expand our life condition.

Also, please remember that your fellow members of the Soka family are always there, ready to share your problems and sufferings and to chant together with you. I am also with you too.

Let's cheerfully usher in a new year of bright promise, with our hearts open and filled with joy!

The World Is
YOUR stage

Future Journal: *Many students have shared their New Year's resolutions with us. They say they want to work overseas or follow your lead in making friends with people around the world.*

President Ikeda: I will continue to pave the way for you throughout the world.

The foundations for worldwide kosen-rufu have been firmly established. All we need now are many more capable people. Please develop yourselves and grow into outstanding leaders. Your development and growth are the hope of humanity.

Spread out the map of the world before you in your mind's eye, unleash your infinite potential, and make this new year [2013] one of great victories.

FJ: *Wherever we go in the world today, we are likely to find SGI members practicing there.*

President Ikeda: It's wonderful, isn't it?

My mentor, Josei Toda, passed the torch of peace to me, saying, "The world is your true stage." I have traveled all around the world on behalf of Mr. Toda, who couldn't do so himself. Making his spirit my own, I have forged friendships around the globe.

President Ikeda in Guam, 1975.

The SGI was established in Guam on January 26, 1975. On that day, I signed my name in the attendance book. In the column for nationality, I wrote, "World." I did so because I firmly believed in the ideal of global citizenship that Mr. Toda had advocated.

Today, the SGI network spans 192 countries and territories—a global network for peace transcending the bounds of nationality and ethnicity. In every corner of the world, our members are well established in their local communities. They are winning trust as good citizens and contributing to society.

FJ: *Some future division members who want to go overseas have asked us what they can do to become global citizens.*

President Ikeda: How admirable! That's an excellent question.

Have you heard the expression "Think globally, act

locally"? That is the essential requirement for becoming a global citizen.

Think globally, act locally.

The American futurist Hazel Henderson, with whom I have spoken many times, made this her slogan as she confronted global environmental problems. She told me that it is not difficult to be a global citizen. In trying to solve global problems, we should do whatever we can in the place where we are right now as fellow inhabitants of planet Earth.

I hope you will all take her words to heart.

What makes us global citizens is our spirit and the actions we take each day.

FJ: *A stay-at-home mother at the time, Ms. Henderson started out by taking action to reduce air pollution in her city.*

President Ikeda: That's right. Fifty years ago, the air in New York City, where she lived, was so polluted that it left a film of soot on your skin when you went outside. She stood up to create a better future for the city's children.

She began by speaking with other mothers she met in a local park. She gained a growing number of supporters and formed a small action group. She wrote letters to the mayor and the TV stations about the problem. She also lodged protests with the big companies who were polluting the air. At first, she was ridiculed as an ignorant housewife, but she refused to give up. She carefully studied the issue, raised public awareness, and worked to see the enactment of laws regulating pollution.

FJ: *The courageous actions of a single individual changed society and led to reform in other parts of the world as well.*

President Ikeda: That's right. The source of Ms. Henderson's courage was the example of her own mother. World War II broke out in Europe when Ms. Henderson was six years old. Britain, where she lived at the time, was subjected to

Hazel Henderson

air raids. Her mother opened their home to people whose houses were destroyed in the bombings.

This noble spirit of mothers to help others even amid their own suffering could be called the very heart of global citizenship.

Actually, all of you have the perfect example of global citizenship right in front of you: your parents and fellow SGI members who practice Nichiren Buddhism. They work day after day for the well-being of others and their communities. They are passionately committed to the great ideal of worldwide kosen-rufu. When they come across someone who is suffering, they share the SGI's inspiring life philosophy with them. They explain the Law of the universe and share personal experiences of revitalizing their lives through their Buddhist practice. They empathize with others, chant with them, and encourage them with their whole heart. None can match their faithful dedication to the happiness of humanity and world peace.

Ms. Henderson also has the highest praise for the SGI movement.

FJ: *A future division member asks what qualities are important to be able, like you, to talk and forge friendships with people from other cultures and religious backgrounds.*

President Ikeda: We can talk about other cultures and so on, but what's important is to realize that we are all human beings. When we see one another as human beings, we can find much common ground. The universal sufferings of birth, aging, sickness, and death concern all thinking people. Studying and practicing Nichiren Buddhism enable us to speak with others heart to heart, at the deepest level of life itself.

Making friends with people from other countries is no different from making friends in your own country. The important thing is to respect others, be honest and open with them, and try to understand them as fellow human beings. Therefore, our behavior is important.

Those who can cheerfully greet and speak to others can be called global citizens. When you greet or speak to someone in a pleasant, friendly way, you can put them at ease and create a warm and receptive atmosphere.

Also, a common characteristic of many of the outstanding international leaders I have met is that they keep their promises. Mr. Toda used to say, "One of the most important habits for young people to develop is keeping promises." Great individuals are honest; they have integrity. Never break your promises to others—or to yourself, for that matter. Making it a policy to always keep your promises will help you become a fine global citizen.

FJ: *Through your citizen's diplomacy, you have forged close friendships between Japan and China, and Japan and Russia.*

President Ikeda: As someone who loves peace, I have done everything I could in my own capacity to promote friendship. When I visited China for the first time in 1974, a little girl came up to me and asked why I was visiting. I said to her, "I have come to meet you!" That was my honest feeling. I wished to become a bridge linking people's hearts. I wanted to bring together people from different countries, especially young people.

After visiting China, I traveled to the former Soviet Union. At the time, many people in Japan were afraid of the Soviet Union. In addition, before my trip, some questioned why I was visiting a nation that had rejected religion. My response was that I was going there to meet people.

I entrust to you, my young successors, the great path of friendship I have built around the globe.

FJ: *At a lecture you delivered at Teachers College, Columbia University, in New York [in 1996], you identified three essential elements of global citizenship: (1) the wisdom to recognize the interconnectedness of all life, (2) the courage not to fear or deny differences but to respect them, and (3) the compassion to empathize with others beyond one's* *immediate surroundings.*[26] *Many people have recognized the importance of these points in terms of resolving the conflicts that continue to plague our world.*

President Ikeda: You are all youthful leaders who will make friends with people around the world and contribute to peace. Please study hard and polish your abilities and characters. Read works of world literature too. We don't read just to get information; we read to gain insight into history and culture of other countries. Reading can also help foster in us a rich spirit of empathy and understanding.

It is my hope, too, that you will learn foreign languages. They are a passport to the world. Don't feel you have to stop at just one foreign language; in the future, being able to speak two or three might be a real asset.

FOREIGN LANGUAGES ARE A PASSPORT TO THE WORLD.

The educator and diplomat Inazo Nitobe aspired in his youth to become a "bridge over the Pacific." He later went on to become a true global citizen, even serving as the under-secretary-general of the League of Nations [forerunner of the United Nations]. He was also, incidentally, an acquaintance of the first Soka Gakkai president, Tsunesaburo Makiguchi.

Nitobe said: "I think that those who take care of their

immediate responsibilities are most commendable. Those who clearly recognize what they need to do now will also come to understand their duty and purpose in life."[27] He believed that cultivating oneself opened the way to the world at large.

If you study hard now and develop greater depth of character, new horizons will open up for you.

The big, wide world is awaiting all of you, my young friends.

FJ: *Some future division members say they have a hard time learning foreign languages.*

President Ikeda: That may have been true until now. But you can always change if you want to, if you make up your mind to really learn. And it is never too late to study and learn.

When I was your age, Japan was at war. English was regarded as an "enemy language," and we were not allowed to study it. I always think that if I could go back to those days, I would try to master a foreign language. That's why I hope you will learn many foreign languages while you are still young and make friends all around the world. Then, if you have the chance, please take your parents overseas as well.

Worldwide kosen-rufu was Nichiren Daishonin's life-long dream. In his writings, there are many references to "Jambudvipa," which means "the entire world."

As young people who uphold and practice the great teaching of Nichiren Buddhism, you are all certain to take your place on the world stage as inspiring global citizens. You will all make wonderful contributions as leaders of society and kosen-rufu.

Looking forward to that day, I will strive alongside all of you again this year. At the start of this new year, let's set forth together with fresh goals, our sights on the future and the world!

Make your lives
TRULY SHINE!

10

Leading a VICTORIOUS Youth Based on Chanting Nam-myoho-renge-kyo

President Ikeda: The days [in February] are still quite chilly, aren't they? I'm always sending prayers to you, my young friends in the future division, so that you won't catch cold. I hope you'll be able to continue your studies in good health and high spirits.

Future Journal: *Many future division members have taken, or will soon be taking, high school or university entrance exams.*[28] *As future division leaders, we will also continue to support them in any way we can.*

Many young members are challenging themselves to recite the sutra and chant Nam-myoho-renge-kyo regularly as they strive to realize their goals or to overcome various personal problems.

President Ikeda: It's wonderful that you are setting goals and chanting to reach them and chanting to overcome your problems. That is how to make your lives truly shine.

Prayer is a sublime act unique to human beings. It is a right and a privilege. Above all, to be able to embrace the Mystic Law—the great Law of the universe—and chant Nam-myoho-renge-kyo at a young age is your supreme fortune. You may not appreciate it fully now, but the time will definitely come when you do.

FJ: *We have received many questions from our readers. For example, some members say they have a hard time believing their parents when they tell them that no prayer to the Gohonzon will go unanswered. Some also want to know why chanting works.*

President Ikeda: In one of his letters, Nichiren Daishonin praises a follower for asking him a frank question about faith. He writes, "For you to inquire about the Lotus Sutra and ask its meaning is a rare source of good fortune" (WND-1, 922). In other words, that you are thinking and asking questions about your Buddhist practice is itself a source of great benefit.

So, why is it that your prayers to the Gohonzon are answered? Because you already have within you the power to actualize your prayers. Your lives are endowed with infinite potential.

Nichiren Buddhism teaches that

> YOUR LIVES ARE *endowed with infinite potential.*

all people, without exception, have the Buddha nature, or the world of Buddhahood.

FJ: High school students who took the Soka Gakkai Study Department entrance exam recently learned about the world of Buddhahood when they studied the Ten Worlds.

Just to refresh everyone's memory, the Ten Worlds are hell, hunger, animality, anger, humanity, heaven, learning, realization, bodhisattva, and Buddhahood. They are the various states of life we have within us.

President Ikeda: That's right.

When you look at your own lives, you can easily see how you go through all different kinds of life states in the course of a single day.

The Daishonin writes, "The sutra texts tell us that a single person in the course of a single day has eight million four thousand thoughts" (WND-2, 307). Our minds are constantly changing in response to various outer and inner conditions.

How can we draw out the strongest, most invincible life state of Buddhahood? The answer, quite simply, is chanting Nam-myoho-renge-kyo to the Gohonzon.

It all starts from there, from our prayer.

FJ: Why does chanting Nam-myoho-renge-kyo cause the state of Buddhahood to emerge?

President Ikeda: Because Nam-myoho-renge-kyo is the "name" of our Buddha nature, or the life state of Buddhahood.

For instance, each of us has our own name. When we hear someone call our name, we turn around and respond, don't we? In the same way, when we chant Nam-myoho-renge-kyo, our Buddhahood says brightly, "I'm here."

In one of his writings, the Daishonin states: "The Buddha nature within us is summoned forth and manifested by our chanting of Nam-myoho-renge-kyo. This is what is meant by 'Buddha'" (WND-1, 887).

Nam-myoho-renge-kyo is the fundamental Law of the universe. It is the ultimate power that drives the movements of the sun and the stars. It exists in the depths of everything in the universe, including our own lives. Therefore, when we chant Nam-myoho-renge-kyo, we can summon forth the positive functions of the universe, which then work to support and protect us.

The Gohonzon is like a window opening on to the universe. Nam-myoho-renge-kyo is the password that activates the Buddhahood of everything in the universe. By chanting, we can tap from within us potential as vast and infinite as the universe itself. We can reveal our true strengths and capabilities—ones that we didn't even realize we had. And nothing is more encouraging than knowing that all the positive forces of the universe are on our side.

This is my conviction as someone who has dedicated his life to spreading Nichiren Buddhism throughout the world as the disciple of Josei Toda. Nothing demonstrates the greatness of the Mystic Law more than that our network of members now extends to 192 countries and territories.

In India, the birthplace of Buddhism, members the same age as you are also chanting Nam-myoho-renge-kyo. In fact, Mahatma Gandhi, who led the way to India's independence, even included Nam-myoho-renge-kyo in the multidenominational prayers he conducted each day at his ashram. I have been told that Gandhi was aware that

Mahatma Gandhi

Nam-myoho-renge-kyo was the ultimate expression of the cosmic power existing within human beings and of the life of the universe itself.[29]

Gandhi, a great champion of nonviolence, began all events and meetings with prayer.

FJ: *You delivered a lecture on Gandhi's life and thought in New Delhi, India [in 1992]. This event took place on February 11, the birthday of Mr. Toda, who cherished the dream of spreading Nichiren Daishonin's teachings throughout Asia.[30]*

President Ikeda: Yes, that's right. In my heart, I dedicated that lecture to Mr. Toda.

Gandhi was a firm believer in the inner power of human beings. Undaunted by government persecution, he remained true to his beliefs, central to which was the power of prayer.

> "PRAYER from the heart can achieve what nothing else can in the world."
>
> –Gandhi

I'd like to share with you these words of Gandhi: "Prayer from the heart can achieve what nothing else can in the world"[31] and "There is no such thing as retreat for a [person] of prayer."[32] For Gandhi, prayer was the mark of true strength. That unwavering conviction made it possible for him to remain optimistic in even the most trying situations. He never stopped believing in a brighter future and the infinite potential of human beings.

In our case, as SGI members with faith in the Mystic Law, Nam-myoho-renge-kyo is the key that allows us to unlock a treasure house of wisdom. The resonance of chanting expands our life limitlessly so that it encompasses the entire universe. It causes courage to surge within us like the rising sun.

Therefore, if we continue to recite the sutra and chant Nam-myoho-renge-kyo, then even when we feel depressed or face discouraging problems, we will be able to recharge our life force and shine in our own unique way.

FJ: *What is the meaning of Nam-myoho-renge-kyo?*

President Ikeda: Each Chinese character in Nam-myoho-renge-kyo has a profound meaning. Nichiren Daishonin explains this in detail in his writings. I hope you'll take time to learn about this someday.

Just as the word Japan includes the entire country, from Hokkaido in the north to Okinawa in the south, Nam-myoho-renge-kyo includes the essence of all Buddhist sutras. Nam-myoho-renge-kyo is the distillation of all laws of the universe, all philosophies, and all the wonders of human existence.

> "There is no true happiness for human beings other than chanting Nam-myoho-renge-kyo."
>
> —Nichiren

In short, Nam-myoho-renge-kyo is the wellspring of eternal hope. It is the flame of invincible fighting spirit. It is the courageous lion's roar of absolute victory. It is the forward-moving rhythm of the universe. And it is the greatest of all joys.

The Gohonzon expresses this in physical form. It is the supreme and unsurpassed mirror of life.

The Daishonin writes, "There is no true happiness for human beings other than chanting Nam-myoho-renge-kyo" (WND-1, 681).

FJ: *It's a fact that even when we're struggling, chanting Nam-myoho-renge-kyo can fill us with incredible energy. It's amazing.*

President Ikeda: From the perspective of the Daishonin's teachings, that is only natural. That's because when we chant, we are repeatedly reaffirming to ourselves, to our own Buddhahood: "My life is precious! I will not be defeated!"

I hope you, my young friends, will not give in to the tendency to devalue yourselves, thinking that you're small and worthless. Because it is not true.

FJ: *Some members have asked how much they should chant.*

President Ikeda: As I have said, chanting is a right, a privilege. So please chant as much as you like, without feeling like it's a burden or duty. There is no specific prescription set down in the Daishonin's teachings for how long we have to chant.

Especially for all of you who are students, studying is your first priority right now. So don't be overly concerned with how much you should chant. Remember that chanting even once has unimaginable power.

If you're in a rush in the morning and only have time to chant Nam-myoho-renge-kyo three times, your intent will still be communicated to the Gohonzon, if you do so sincerely. And all the chanting you do in addition to that will accumulate in your life as good fortune. It will be a deposit in the "bank of the universe," as it were, that will stand you in good stead when you need it.

FJ: *Some members have said that they can't concentrate when they chant because their minds wander or that they hurry through chanting because they want to watch TV.*

President Ikeda: That is why chanting is called a "practice." If you have the spirit to keep challenging yourself to chant, or if you have a goal that you truly want to achieve, then you'll naturally get into the habit of chanting seriously. Just challenge yourself in your own way.

Setting clear goals will motivate you to chant more seriously. You're young, so it's important to set detailed, concrete goals that will enable you to grow as a person.

Set Clear Goals

When I was young, I constantly struggled with illness. I also had to deal with the financial crisis that enveloped Mr. Toda's businesses. Resolving to use those challenges as opportunities to test the power of Nam-myoho-renge-kyo, I chanted my hardest and made all-out efforts. As a result, I surmounted every difficulty and gained the absolute conviction that no prayer to the Gohonzon goes unanswered and that nothing is more powerful than chanting Nam-myoho-renge-kyo.

FJ: *Some members say that no matter how hard they chant, their prayers aren't answered.*

President Ikeda: If you keep chanting seriously, everything will certainly move in a positive direction.

Prayer in Nichiren Buddhism is a vow. It is a pledge to realize your wish without fail. When you strengthen your resolve, you're able to work wholeheartedly. And because of your efforts, you can become the kind of people who can make their prayers come true. Buddhism, above all, is reason. It is not some mysterious, magical power.

Another purpose of our Buddhist practice is to achieve human revolution. If all your wishes came true immediately, you might think that things will work out somehow, even if you don't make any effort. Then you would never really grow as a person.

If you chant and make effort, your deepest desires will surely be fulfilled. Those who chant powerfully and consistently will ultimately experience a victorious youth and a triumphant life. It will be greater than any they ever imagined. Therefore, please don't allow yourself to be defeated by momentary sadness or suffering because something didn't go the way you'd hoped. Don't be impatient.

Life is filled with all sorts of challenges, including illness, financial hardship, and relationship problems. But when we continue to chant Nam-myoho-renge-kyo, we can transform every struggle into a wonderful story of happiness and victory. The day will definitely come when you can look back and say, "That hardship made me who I am today." That's what our Buddhist practice is for.

I hope all of you, my young friends, will set big goals, keep chanting to realize them, and take action to make them a reality. I will join with you in chanting for this each day.

I continually pray that each one of you will walk the path to victory in your youth, brimming with confidence and joy.

11

You CAN Do It!

President Ikeda: In Japan, March is a time of fresh, hope-filled departures.[33] Nothing delights me more than to see you, our future division members, growing at such an astonishing rate and taking on new challenges.

Future Journal: *Over the past year, future division members have enjoyed reading this series and carrying on a conversation with you in their hearts. As future division leaders, we've learned many things about the mentor-disciple spirit from these young members.*

President Ikeda: That's wonderful! All of you, the members and the leaders of the future division, are always in my heart.

I receive reports each day from future division members in different areas. They write how they are challenging themselves in their studies, in reading, in extracurricular activities, and in future division activities. They also say they are trying hard to make friends and to show their appreciation to their parents.

You future division members are all champions who never stop making efforts.

Allow me to congratulate those of you who will be graduating from junior high or high school this March. I commend you on completing three years[34] of hard work.

I would like to especially praise those of you living in areas affected by the devastating March 2011 earthquake and tsunami in the Tohoku area. I know you must have overcome many hardships and challenges. I hope that, with the support of your family and friends, you will continue to overcome every obstacle. I will chant for your happiness, success, and victory in life and watch over you as long as I live.

FJ: *The graduating girls will soon join the ranks of the young women's division.*

President Ikeda: Yes. When they do, they'll find that they have friends all around the world. We live in a truly remarkable age of worldwide kosen-rufu.

Also, please remember that no matter what direction you may choose to follow after you graduate, we will always share a connection. I hope each of you will keep polishing your young life in a way that is true to yourself, with optimism and in good health.

In Japan, March is traditionally known as Yayoi, a name that suggests the new growth of plants in spring. I, therefore, hope each of you will take your place on the new stage that lies before you—like fresh green shoots emerging after the winter cold and like flowers blossoming to announce the arrival of spring.

FJ: Some graduating from junior high or high school this spring say they feel sad about having to part with friends.

President Ikeda: Yes, that can be hard. But real friendship is something we continue to nurture all our lives. Even if you and your friends take separate paths, you can keep encouraging one another. You and your friends are still young. The important thing is to look to the future together and move ahead with a positive, upbeat spirit.

Many new friends are waiting for you as well.

Don't let your sadness overwhelm you, but please live your youth joyfully, wisely, and with a true richness of heart. Cherish all the positive relationships you make in your life.

In particular, graduation is a chance for you to reaffirm how much you owe to all those in your life who have helped and supported you until now. It's a chance to deepen your relationships.

I hope you will express your sincerest thanks to your parents, relatives, teachers, and friends, as well as the members of your local Soka family.

FJ: Some students who will be entering their final year of junior high or high school worry about living up to the standards of their predecessors in clubs, student government, and so forth.

In addition, some who will soon become high school division leaders are wondering how they'll be able to inspire their fellow members.

President Ikeda: There's no need to worry! It's only natural to be a little anxious at first. That just shows how much you care for others, how responsible you feel. That, in itself, shows a wonderful leadership spirit. It's also an important part of personal development.

Remember, each of you is unique. You can't behave exactly as those before you did, and there's no need to. You'll be able to blaze a trail if you do your best in your own way, while of course maintaining any good traditions.

More importantly, you all uphold the Mystic Law. By chanting seriously and turning all hardships into joy, you cannot fail to develop into trustworthy seniors and capable leaders.

FJ: *Some members say they're reluctant to step up to take the lead. They worry that taking on leadership will consume all their time. Others hesitate to shoulder heavy responsibilities.*

President Ikeda: True, responsibility can sound rather burdensome. But when you actually take it on, you give yourself a great opportunity to push beyond your limits.

Konosuke Matsushita was the founder of Panasonic, hailed by many as a business genius. I met him on several occasions. I fondly recall talking with him for four or five hours each time about various aspects of life. We ultimately published a dialogue together.[35]

Mr. Matsushita was also an expert at fostering people. Allow me to share a story with you.

Back in the late 1920s, electric clothes irons were quite expensive. Convenient as they were, most people couldn't afford them. So one day Mr. Matsushita said to a young technician, "I want to manufacture an electric iron that's as inexpensive as possible, so everyone can enjoy the convenience of using one."

The young man agreed that was a good idea and asked who would be in charge of the project.

"You," Mr. Matsushita said. "I want you to be in charge."

Without the knowledge or necessary experience, the man rejected the idea. He said it would be impossible for him to do it on his own. But Mr. Matsushita countered without a moment's hesitation: "No, you can do it. I know you can."

In response to Mr. Matsushita's confidence in him, the young man summoned all his creativity and ingenuity. He developed an iron that was as good as the expensive ones but much lower in price. It was of such high quality that it was designated as an Excellent Domestic Product by the Japanese Ministry of Commerce and Industry at the time.

FJ: *Mr. Matsushita recognized the young man's potential.*

President Ikeda: That's right. He saw the hidden potential the young man himself didn't even know he had. Later, that technician became a top executive in the company. He later recalled: "Those few words, 'You can do it,' ignited a fire in my heart."

Mr. Matsushita believed in this young man and entrusted him with a mission. That trust lit the flame of responsibility in his young heart. Young people need to resolve to themselves: "I will do it. I will definitely accomplish my goal." Once you decide to achieve something, a strength you never knew you had will well up from within.

I would like to share some of Mr. Matsushita's words:

"The key to success is to keep trying until you achieve your goal."

–Konosuke Matsushita

"Instead of worrying that you'll fail or assuming you can't do something, it's important to have the confidence and tenacity to believe that you can do it if you try and that, if you fail, you'll learn what you can from it and try again."[36] He also said, "The key to success is to keep trying until you achieve your goal."[37]

Mr. Matsushita experienced numerous business crises, but he always managed to get back on his feet again. He believed that a business is only as good as its employees. So he devoted himself to fostering people by entrusting them with important tasks. His health was frail, but he never gave up. He kept striving for the sake of his companies, his employees and their families, and the prosperity of Japan and the world.

A sense of responsibility is another name for personal commitment and persistence.

FJ: *Mr. Matsushita visited both Soka University in Tokyo and the Soka Girls Junior High and High Schools in Osaka (in 1975).*

President Ikeda: Yes, he was very dedicated to education. He was thirty years my senior, of the same generation as my mentor, Mr. Toda. I showed him around our schools as if I were welcoming my mentor.

At the Soka schools in Osaka, he was treated to a performance by the fife and drums corps. Afterward, he walked up to the performers and repeatedly thanked them with a broad smile.

I'll never forget the words he shared with me after interacting with the students. He said with great emphasis: "I feel as if I've grown ten or twenty years younger today! I would give my entire fortune to be young again. But that's not possible. In place of that, I have received a powerful dose of youthful energy from the Soka students."

You all have this supremely precious treasure of youth. Being young is in itself a truly wonderful thing. You need have no fear of anything.

Mr. Toda also cherished young people. He had absolute faith in their pure-hearted commitment to their ideals, their great passion for truth and justice, and their potential for limitless growth.

FJ: *March 16, Kosen-rufu Day, the anniversary of the day when President Toda passed the baton of mentor and disciple on to the youth is fast approaching.*

President Ikeda: On March 16, 1958, some six thousand of us youth division members gathered around Mr. Toda for a ceremony in which he entrusted kosen-rufu to us, his successors of the next generation. Some of those who assembled that day were the same age as you, our future division members.

That solemn ceremony of mentor and disciple signified the momentous declaration that youth are the protagonists of kosen-rufu. Having always been at Mr. Toda's side, I fully understood his feelings on that day.

We, the young people, inherited Mr. Toda's spirit and recognized our own missions. We stirred up a groundswell of human revolution. We did not let any form of persecution defeat us, and we surmounted every difficulty for the sake of Mr. Toda and kosen-rufu. We regard this as our greatest honor in life.

Nichiren Daishonin says, "Form your ranks and follow me" (WND-1, 765). You, my young friends, are the ones who will stand up and take the lead for the development of worldwide kosen-rufu in the future. Here and now, I solemnly present the baton of the mentor-disciple spirit to you, our future division members.

Josei Toda entrusts the youth with the future of kosen-rufu, March 16, 1958.

FJ: *You once told the future division, "When you awaken to your mission, your innate abilities will quickly blossom."*

President Ikeda: In Japanese, the word for *mission* is written with two Chinese characters meaning "to use one's life." To what use should we put our lives?—this is a question we must continue to ask ourselves.

Mission isn't something apart from your everyday lives. If you challenge each task or obstacle you face, you will eventually discover your unique purpose in life. At some point, you will know, "This is my mission!" Therefore, there's no need to be impatient.

You all have within you limitless strength to move forward, become happy, and win. All you need to do is face each of your problems head-on, study hard, and develop yourselves. Make full use of all your youthful energy.

Whatever anyone else may say, I believe in you. I believe in you completely. When you feel weighed down by the load of your worries and fears, please chant to the Gohonzon with your honest feelings.

Though there may be times when you want to give up on yourself, I never will. I have always kept on fighting right through to the very end, never giving up, and I continue to do so to this day. Therefore, no matter what challenges you might be facing, I confidently say to you,

"You can do it!"

"LET'S GET STARTED
on a path of fresh challenges
and victories together!"

CHALLENGE
Yourselves and Grow

President Ikeda: Congratulations to everyone starting junior high and high school this year!

Your family is praying for your growth. Your leaders and other SGI members are all supporting you. I am also chanting for you each day. Let's get started on a path of fresh challenges and victories together!

Future Journal: *Many new junior high school students are reading this series for the first time.*

President Ikeda: That's wonderful! I am taking part in this series as if I were engaging in a one-to-one conversation with each of you.

I look forward to the many letters I receive from you each month. I am always thinking about the problems and struggles you are facing. I would like to explore and work through them together with you.

If you find some parts of our dialogue hard to understand, feel free to skip over them. I will be happy if you learn even one thing that you can apply to your life.

FJ: *Some readers have said that as they start a new school year, they worry about making friends or about not fitting in.*

President Ikeda: Most people feel the same way, so please don't worry too much.

I remember something that happened around the time of my first visit to China, nearly forty years ago. It was just after diplomatic relations between China and Japan had been restored. The young people who were to accompany me were intent on cramming as much knowledge about China into their heads as possible. In Japan at the time, not much was known about China. So the youth were all rather nervous and bracing themselves for their visit there.

I was pleased by their wish to study beforehand. But I said: "Let's just experience China as it is, without preconceived notions, and do our best to make friends! As fellow human beings and youth, let's open our hearts to people there. Let's talk to them, learn from one another, and build trust." And as I hoped, many friendships were formed on that trip.

As you start the school year, don't judge the people you meet. Just start by casually greeting them when you see them. You may be surprised to find how much you have in common.

FJ: *Some students say that they are more anxious than excited by the prospect of starting a new school year. How can they overcome this anxiety?*

President Ikeda: It's only natural to feel nervous in a new environment. Don't try to force yourself not to be.

But it's important to take some sort of action. Don't be passive. Take the initiative and try to do something about it. Once you take that first step, you'll find your anxiety gradually fading.

Finding yourself in a new environment is a chance to make a fresh start—a chance to boldly take on new challenges.

As you make this new start, I would like to share some words from Rosa Parks. My wife and I cherished her as a dear friend. She said, "In order to bring about change, one must not be afraid to take the first step, or else it will not be done."[38] She also said, "The only failure is failing to try."[39]

"The only failure is failing to try."
-Rosa Parks

FJ: *Mrs. Parks fought against racial discrimination and is known as the "mother of the American Civil Rights Movement."*

In some parts of the United States in the mid-1950s, African Americans were required to give up their seats to white people

*on public buses. One day, Mrs. Parks refused to do so and was
arrested. Her courageous stand led to the Montgomery Bus
Boycott, a pivotal event that transformed history.*

President Ikeda: Mrs. Parks was a great person, a champion committed to peace. She also deeply loved the world's children. I have a wonderful memory of singing the anthem of the Civil Rights Movement, "We Shall Overcome," with her and the young people who were on hand to welcome her at our first meeting [in Los Angeles in 1993].

As a child, Mrs. Parks had a hard time because she was sickly and unable to attend school every day. Still, she refused to let that defeat her. For a time, she received lessons at home from her mother and grandmother, and she grew to love learning and reading.

Some years later, when she was in high school, her grandmother became ill. Mrs. Parks was forced to drop out of school to nurse her. Later, when she tried to return to high school, her mother fell ill. She spent her youth wanting to study but being unable to do so to her heart's content.

Even so, she didn't give up. After marrying at a young age, she set a goal to graduate from high school. Her efforts paid off, and she finally received her high school diploma.

The greatness of Mrs. Parks lies in her spirit to always follow through on her goals, no matter what, and to boldly challenge herself.

FJ: *It's important to challenge yourself, regardless of your circumstances.*

President Ikeda: That's right. Nichiren Daishonin states: "There is definitely something extraordinary in . . . the way in which summer, autumn, winter, and spring give way to each other. Something uncommon also occurs when an ordinary person attains Buddhahood" (WND-1, 637).

In Japan, when winter gives way to spring, a strong warm wind from the south usually marks the change of season. Although the strong winds can be unpleasant, they are actually happy tidings that spring will soon arrive.

The same is true in our lives. Anxiety, suffering, and problems are all signs of personal growth. As the expression goes, "No pain, no gain."

Don't let the winds of anxiety hold you back. Press ahead one step at a time. There's no need to rush or to compare yourself to others. Just confidently follow your own path, in your own unique way.

FJ: *A reader says that he wants to take on a fresh challenge with the start of the new school year, but he can't decide what it should be.*

President Ikeda: How honest. Simply wanting to try something new is itself wonderful.

Taking on a new challenge and striving to improve yourself doesn't mean you have to do anything extraordinary. If you get all wrapped up in chasing some fantastic dream but lose sight of who you are, then it would be such a waste.

To really grow, it's crucial to have a firm foundation. Steady, consistent efforts are essential. It is also important to have the courage to keep challenging yourself. Make a start with something doable and progress a little at a time.

Right now, the Soka Gakkai's new headquarters is under construction. Work started the year before last, in 2011, and a fine new building will be completed in November this year [2013]. The fact is that the greatest amount of time was spent on the building's foundation.

Towering Mount Fuji stands so regal and serene because of its enormous base. A cherry tree blooms beautifully because its roots reach deep into the earth. The same is true of people. Outstanding individuals always have a strong foundation. That's why I want all of you to have solid foundations and win in your daily lives.

The Hall of the Great Vow, Tokyo.

Paying attention to getting the basics right is the key to winning in life and developing admirable character. This could include such mundane things as greeting people when you see them, taking good care of your health, or being organized in morning so that you don't forget things or arrive late to school.

I hope you will also challenge yourselves to chant.

Chanting nourishes our spirit. It's the way to polish and forge our lives. The time we spend chanting is a precious time when we can align our lives with the rhythm of the universe.

FJ: *Another reader expresses the wish to change but doesn't know how.*

President Ikeda: Start by setting goals. The important thing in setting goals is to make them as concrete as you can. You can write them down on a piece of paper and paste it up somewhere where you'll see it.

You may set a vague goal, like "Read more good books." But you may find that, as time passes, your resolve starts to fade. You may lose interest in even opening a book and forget that you even had any books!

But if you make your goal specific, such as, "This month I will read this particular book," you can figure out how many pages you need to read each day to finish it. You will also be able to find a practical way to do it—say, for instance, going to school ten minutes earlier each day and using that time for reading.

When you reach the goal you set for the day, you will have written another page in the story of your human revolution. You will feel that you are growing and changing little by little. You will gain the self-confidence that you can succeed if you try. And this will make you want to take up the next challenge.

Nichiren writes, "The situation is like the joints in a

piece of bamboo: if one joint is ruptured, then all the joints will split" (WND-1, 512). When you break through one obstacle, you gain powerful momentum.

It's important that you set your own goals and strive to achieve them in your own way. There is no need to compare yourself to others or play down your own efforts. Set goals that you want to achieve; that will give you a sense of accomplishment.

President Makiguchi declared, "An arrow aimed at a vague target will not hit its mark."[40] In our prayers and in our personal challenges, being specific is all-important.

FJ: *Some students say they feel depressed because they didn't get accepted into the school of their choice.*

President Ikeda: That is certainly disappointing. It is only natural that you might feel down. But life is long. From the long-term perspective, that disappointment may lead to great growth and victory.

Even though you didn't get in, that doesn't change the fact that you tried. Young people who are not defeated by setbacks but who use them as opportunities to challenge themselves again can lead a youth that shines with victory.

I founded the Soka schools and Soka University because I wanted to foster young people who would have this challenging spirit. All those who have taken an entrance exam for those schools with a challenging spirit are Soka students, whether they were accepted or not. They are equally precious to me. As the schools' founder, I applaud them sincerely, and I will always watch over them and chant for them.

I hope that all of you will fully enjoy your time at whatever school you attend. Feel pride and joy to be where you are. You can all do that, I am certain. I'm confident that you can be fulfilled each day and become proud, smiling graduates.

Spring is a time for brightly, energetically, and positively making a fresh start filled with courage and hope.

It's spring! Let's start fresh! Let's begin an adventure of discovering a new self! My young friends, be joyful champions of challenge and effort!

13

Shine Brightly and ILLUMINATE the World!

Future Journal: *Spring has arrived in Japan. Congratulations on May 3, Soka Gakkai Day!*

President Ikeda: Congratulations! I am delighted to celebrate May 3 with all of you, future division members throughout the world. Nothing makes me happier than to see you shining brightly and growing vigorously, like the green leaves of May.

FJ: *May 3 is the starting point of the Soka Gakkai. On that day in 1951, Josei Toda was inaugurated as the second Soka Gakkai president and vowed to achieve a membership of 750,000 households.*

President Ikeda: At that time, we had only about three thousand members. Achieving a membership of 750,000 households seemed impossible to most people. But I took Mr. Toda's vow as my own and got to work. I went everywhere to encourage members who were suffering, and one by one, they stood up together with me. A single ripple became ten thousand waves, and my mentor's goal of 750,000 households was achieved.

FJ: *On May 3, 1960, following in President Toda's footsteps, you were inaugurated as the third Soka Gakkai president. In the more than half century since then, you have traveled the globe with the aim of achieving kosen-rufu—namely, peace and happiness for all humanity.*

President Ikeda: Today, the SGI network has spread to 192 countries and territories. The chanting of Nam-myoho-renge-kyo can be heard on this planet twenty-four hours a day, 365 days a year. I know this would make Mr. Toda extremely happy.

May 3 is also Soka Gakkai Mother's Day. I proposed this significant day to celebrate and express our profound thanks to our women's division members—the hard-working mothers of kosen-rufu. I hope you, my young friends, will offer special thanks on this day to your mothers for all that they do for you.

The renowned environmental activist and Nobel Peace laureate Dr. Wangari Maathai was deeply grateful to her mother all her life. Dr. Maathai is well known for promoting the maternal spirit of caring for life and the environment. The slogan of *mottainai* ("What a waste!"), which she adopted from Japanese, became a symbol of this spirit. Its underlying message is respect for nature and not wasting the planet's precious resources.

Dr. Maathai, who was a dear friend of mine and my wife's, sent me a video message with her congratulations on the fiftieth anniversary of my inauguration [on May 3, 2010]. I'll never forget her bright, warm smile as she said in the video that there had not been one place in her travels around the world where she had not met a happy SGI member. She added that they all seemed so happy that the word *happy* itself made her think of SGI members.

Today, joyful SGI members are active in every corner of the world. We have truly entered a wonderful age.

FJ: *One high school student asked us why it is that the SGI movement has spread so widely around the world.*

President Ikeda: That's a very good question. The answer is that we focus on valuing and encouraging each person.

Whenever we learn of fellow members who are struggling, we hurry to their side and encourage them. We chant with them, help them find a positive perspective, and support them as they challenge their situation. With a fresh sense of hope they gain through this process, they then go on to encourage others.

Our network, which spans 192 countries and territories, has been built through an endless chain of encouragement from one person to another and through countless dramas of human revolution. This is the essence of our movement. The SGI places the highest value on each individual.

And playing a central role in our movement are your dedicated mothers and other women, who are as noble and as worthy of respect as Buddhas.

FJ: *Several members have asked how to convey the greatness of the SGI to their friends.*

President Ikeda: That's wonderful. Wanting to share Nichiren Buddhism with friends is truly admirable.

There is no formula or script for telling others about Nichiren Buddhism and the SGI. Just honestly share what you feel from chanting, attending discussion meetings, and participating in future division activities.

You can say that there are a lot of nice people; that everyone is positive and energetic; that when you chant, you feel courage welling up from within; that Buddhism is very profound—whatever you feel. There is no need to overthink it.

Actually, the best way to convey the greatness of Nichiren Buddhism is for you yourselves to shine your brightest.

Right now, as junior high and high school students, please concentrate on your studies and making friends. You don't have to go out of your way to talk about the SGI. Your efforts in school and elsewhere will be actual proof of how wonderful our organization is. Your warm concern for your friends will embody the philosophy of the SGI. Your shining faces, your courageous examples of challenging yourselves, your invincible spirit, and your caring voices as you encourage others will brighten those around you as does the sun.

I'd like to share with you the words of the French author Romain Rolland: "The goodness of a single good person illuminates all humanity. The good or evil of humanity as a whole therefore depends on each of us as an individual."[41]

The SGI is indeed illuminating humanity with the light of good.

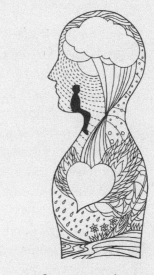

"The goodness of a single good person illuminates all humanity."

–Romain Rolland

FJ: *Rolland's novel* **Jean-Christophe** *and his biography of Beethoven are often read by young people in Japan.*

President Ikeda: Romain Rolland lived at the same time as Mr. Makiguchi. When Rolland was a boy, France's defeat in the Franco-Prussian War and other circumstances cast a pall over his country. But he found hope in books and became an avid reader who studied hard.

Rolland opposed war based on his philosophy of love for all humankind. He was an activist writer who called out for peace without fearing persecution.

I read his books when I was young too. Japan was a gloomy and turbulent place after its defeat in World War II. In those times, Rolland's works, masterpieces of the human spirit, were a great source of hope. They announced a new dawn of peace and freedom.

FJ: *In a speech at Soka University once, you shared some quotes from* **Jean-Christophe**, *including, "Even suffering is joy if it be shared."*[42] *And you emphasized that friendship is a life-long treasure.*

President Ikeda: Nothing in this world is more precious or true than friendship. Based on that belief, I have through dialogue built bridges linking people around the world and created an expansive network of friendship.

As a youth, Rolland was deeply impressed by the works of the Russian author Leo Tolstoy. He even exchanged letters with him. He also built friendships with the champion of nonviolence Mahatma Gandhi; the poet Rabindranath Tagore; the physicist and peace advocate Albert Einstein; and the physician and humanitarian Albert Schweitzer, who selflessly dedicated himself to providing medical care to people in Africa.

Rolland wanted to bring the world together through

friendship. He wanted to create an alliance of goodness that could overcome prejudice and hatred. His dream is now being made a reality by the SGI's movement for peace, culture, and education.

FJ: *That is an inspiring thought. I'm sure what you've just said will be helpful to members who've said they have difficulty answering their friends' questions about what the SGI does.*

President Ikeda: That your friends ask you questions about the SGI shows that they trust you. The SGI is an international organization and is active on many fronts. It is not easy to quickly sum up all of our activities.

Put simply, the SGI is a gathering of individuals who practice Nichiren Buddhism out of a wish for the happiness of all people. You could say that the

SGI is working to invigorate and brighten the world.

Buddhism shows through our actions. It comes to life in our relationships. And the essence of these interactions is to encourage one another.

Take the example of our members in Tohoku. Despite having their lives turned upside down in the devastating March 2011 earthquake and tsunami, they continue to help and encourage others. They have inspired many people and shine with the true Soka Gakkai spirit.

To reach out to and warmly encourage those who are suffering, to accompany them on the path to happiness—such actions shine with genuine humanity. To take such action is to live the most correct way of life. If you look at those in your own family who practice Nichiren Buddhism, as well as the SGI members around you, you'll see that this is so.

FJ: *Some members have said that they feel terrible when their friends talk badly about the SGI.*

President Ikeda: People say those things precisely because we are doing the right thing.

Nichiren Daishonin writes, "To be praised by fools— that is the greatest shame" (WND-1, 287). And in the same vein, President Makiguchi said, "To be despised by fools is the greatest honor."

At the Kansai Soka Junior High and High Schools, I once spoke about an episode from Romain Rolland's life: In his student days, Rolland stood up for a friend who was being bullied by classmates. The attackers criticized him for doing so, but he held fast to his convictions. He continued to protect his friend and dismissed the bullies. He encouraged his friend, saying, "Let us continue ahead on our chosen path."[43]

Rolland and his friend became a source of inspiration for each other and both became renowned writers.[44]

In its early days, the Soka Gakkai was ridiculed as "a gathering of the poor and sick." People told members who were trying to share Nichiren Buddhism: "Come back when you're healed!" or "I'll start practicing when you get rich!" But our members kept pressing onward, no matter what people said.

As they bravely carried out their Buddhist practice, they did overcome their illnesses and turn their lives around, becoming truly happy. And they did not just practice for themselves. They prayed for their friends'

happiness and contributed to their communities and societies. They thereby achieved a life state of supreme victory. This brilliant history of human revolution is the great pride of the SGI. The members of the SGI are noble beyond measure.

Today, leaders in various fields around the world have the highest praise for the SGI's success in fostering outstanding young people who contribute to society. Good-hearted, thinking people everywhere have become allies of the SGI.

FJ: *Some people ask what they should give priority to when the schedule for SGI activities clashes with extracurricular activities or gatherings with friends.*

President Ikeda: Of course, you are free to make your own decisions. It is good training for you to have to decide which activity has more value for you at that moment in your life. You can also consult with your parents or your seniors in the organization, if you like.

Remember that SGI meetings always give you something of value. You usually leave feeling energized. Even if you aren't aware of it at that moment, something remains with you, in your life. Years from now, you'll really appreciate having gone to meetings during your youth.

Even so, there are probably going to be times when you decide to give priority to spending time with friends, doing extracurricular activities, or playing sports. Faith is for a lifetime, so you don't need to view things narrowly.

Faith is for a lifetime ...

You are the protagonists of the future. You are the ones who will build the next generation of the SGI. If May 3 is the eternal starting point of the Soka Gakkai, then May 5, Soka Gakkai Successors Day, is the day of eternal hope. I pray and have confidence that you will lead lives of happiness and victory.

14

Make Good Books Your
COMPANIONS

Future Journal: *June is here, marking the start of summer, and our junior high and high school division members are excited.*

President Ikeda: June is also the month when the rainy season begins in Japan. I hope you will take extra care of your health during the changes of weather.

Nichiren Daishonin writes, "Strengthen your faith day by day and month after month" (WND-1, 997). Faith is about having the spirit to keep moving forward, just like a flowing stream, year in and year out.

FJ: *Yes, we'll do our best. The constant rain, however, can be a bit of a drag . . . .*

President Ikeda: That may be true. But rain causes plants and trees to flourish. It makes the flowers that grow this time of year, the hydrangeas and pomegranate flowers, glisten beautifully. And how refreshing the breeze when it stops raining! Depending on your outlook, the rain can be enjoyable and uplifting.

FJ: *As you say, hydrangeas are particularly beautiful in the rainy season, blooming in various colors.*

President Ikeda: I have photographed hydrangeas many times. Hydrangeas can change their color depending on the acidity of the soil. This image of hydrangeas, which absorb different kinds of nourishment and grow vigorously to the delight of all who see them, reminds me of you, the future division members.

I hope that all of you will absorb rich spiritual nourishment and bring your own unique flowers of mission into bloom. I also hope you become people who can work for the happiness of many others.

FJ: *Reading is a great source of spiritual nourishment. Many of the questions sent in relate to reading.*

President Ikeda: Yes, reading is very important. It is a springboard for victory in your youth. It also helps form the foundation for the rest of your life. It is a source of knowledge and wisdom. It is a training ground that allows you to expand your horizons, enrich your spirit, and exercise your mind.

Books are tickets to far-flung destinations. They can instantly take you to any place in the world. You can visit every continent, go to the North and South Poles, and even travel into outer space.

Books are wonderful and handy time machines. They

can transport you into the future or back to the past—to the time of rival warlords during the Three Kingdoms period in China or to the time of Joan of Arc in France.

Reading books can also be an opportunity to converse with great individuals. You can become friends with Goethe and Tolstoy, with Nightingale and Curie. You can receive encouragement from Mahatma Gandhi and Martin Luther King Jr.

Books enable you to transcend time and space and experience worlds of unknown dimensions.

Books enable you to transcend time and space and experience worlds of unknown dimensions. And you don't need to pack or save lots of money for the trip!

As long as you have a book, a new world can open up before your eyes, at any time or place. It is a treasure you all have within easy reach.

FJ: *Some say they find reading difficult. Their parents tell them to read, but they get bored quickly.*

President Ikeda: Trying things that are hard for you is admirable. That's all you need to do. Just keep challenging yourself. Someday you'll come to enjoy reading.

It is okay to put down a book in the middle, if it bores you. It's fine if you start reading something and then decide you don't like it and put it back on the shelf. Your unread books will wait for you!

If you want to read a different book, go ahead. Sometimes you'll find, years later, that you can breeze through a book that once gave you trouble. Everyone has their own way of interacting with books. Don't overthink it. The main thing is to get into the habit of exposing yourself to books, even a little.

It's also important to find books you might actually like to read. You can go to the library or a bookstore, or you can look over the reviews and ads for books in newspapers or on the internet. You can also ask your friends what they're reading and what they found interesting.

By browsing for books and talking about them, you'll find your interest piqued. Eventually, you're sure to come across a book you really want to read.

Remember, reading good books will definitely contribute to your growth and self-improvement.

FJ: *In some cases, junior high and high school students can't do a lot of reading for various reasons. They're studying for exams or are simply too tired from extracurricular activities.*

President Ikeda: In that case, just keep adding to the list of books you want to read. You can then read them later. You have your whole life to do so. The more you read, the more your life will be enriched. For me, to read is to live and to live is to read.

I'd like to share with you some words of the Russian author and playwright Anton Chekhov, whom I studied in my youth with my mentor: "With each new page I read in a book, my life becomes richer, stronger, and better."[45]

FJ: Chekhov is known as the author of such famous plays as **The Cherry Orchard** *and* **The Seagull**. *When he was young, his family went bankrupt. He started writing for magazines to help support his family when he was at college.*

Pʀᴇꜱɪᴅᴇɴᴛ Iᴋᴇᴅᴀ: From the time he was a boy, Chekhov helped out in the grocery store his father ran. During that time, he never had any vacation or enough time to study. He was often sick too. After his father's grocery store went bankrupt, he continued his high school education while working as a tutor. He was just sixteen.

But he had one pleasure—going to the new library and reading. He was so engrossed in reading Hugo, Schopenhauer, and others that he sometimes forgot to eat! Reading in those difficult times strengthened his spirit and improved his academic ability. Eventually, he wrote numerous works that enthralled people around the world.

FJ: You also read many books in your youth when you were living through hard times.

Pʀᴇꜱɪᴅᴇɴᴛ Iᴋᴇᴅᴀ: I was seventeen when World War II ended. It was a time when values in Japan had collapsed. Young people were searching for the best way to live and the true meaning of happiness. I avidly read great works of literature in my quest for answers. I worked despite my poor health, and I saved up little by little so I could go to the used bookstore. I can still remember the joy I felt when I could buy a book I wanted.

Even after I went to work for Mr. Toda, I continued my reading. I made all-out efforts to get his businesses back on a sound footing. But I still tried to keep broadening my knowledge through reading. No matter how tired I was when I got home at night, I always opened a book.

Whenever Mr. Toda saw me, he would ask, "Daisaku, what are you reading now?" Or he'd want to know if I'd ever read this or that book. He would then tell me to summarize it and share with him my impressions. This was all valuable training. Mr. Toda taught me the true significance of reading and enabled me to cultivate real strength.

Mr. Toda was jailed along with his mentor, Mr. Makiguchi, for opposing Japan's militarist authorities during the war. The conditions in prison were terrible, but they both continued to read. Despite his advanced age, Mr. Makiguchi still burned with a passion for self-improvement; right up to his death in prison, he was reading the philosophy of Immanuel Kant. Mr. Toda, too, requested his family to bring many books to him in jail.

We can learn anywhere. I hope you will study hard and read as many good books as you possibly can.

FJ: *Some members say they are too busy to read.*

President Ikeda: It's true junior high and high school students these days are very busy. But reading isn't a matter of having spare time. Many extremely busy people are also often great readers. Indeed, all of the world leaders and thinkers I've met read books amid their incredibly busy schedules.

If you are busy, it is important that you find just a few moments and use them valuably. For example, you might read while riding on the train, or for ten minutes in the morning, or for five minutes while waiting for someone.

I used to go to a cemetery to read. It was really quiet there!

At any rate, many small efforts to read can accumulate over time into a great treasure. It's important to try, even if you can only read a page or a few lines at a time. Each time you do so, your life will become richer and stronger, as Chekhov said.

> It's important to try, even if you can only read a page or a few lines at a time.

One way to start is to always carry a book with you. Then, whenever you have a spare minute, you can pull it out and read. You can make the most of the time you have, even if it's limited.

FJ: *Students have also asked what kind of books they should read. They wonder how they can make best use of their reading time. Others say that there are many books they want to read but because they are slow readers it takes them a long time to get through even one.*

President Ikeda: Once reading becomes second nature, I hope you'll try to read great works of world literature. Mr. Toda always used to urge me to read lengthy novels and the classics. The great works that have stood the test of time shine as inexhaustible wellsprings of philosophy and wisdom. I guarantee that they will be a wonderful asset for your lives.

You can also get suggestions from your future division leaders and your teachers. Those who thoughtfully read even one great work can access an invaluable reservoir of human wisdom and find tremendous hope. It is like gaining a lifelong friend.

FJ: *Today almost everyone uses the internet or cell phones. We are exposed to the written word, in the broadest sense, more and more. Some say that we spend so much time with words and information that we don't need to go out of our way to read books.*

President Ikeda: Of course, it's important to keep abreast of the news. But most important is to cultivate your ability to think and, by extension, the ability to express yourself. Instead of being manipulated by information, I hope you will take it in, make the best use of it, and learn to express your own thoughts and feelings.

Mr. Toda always encouraged young people to make time for reading and deep thinking in their lives.

Great works of literature are the shared treasures of humanity. If you read them seriously and etch their messages in your lives, you will be able to hold your own in a conversation with virtually anyone.

FJ: *I am reminded of how you once sent a message to former Soviet president Mikhail Gorbachev at a difficult time for him [in 1991]. You told him to take to heart these words from Chekhov's* **The Cherry Orchard***: "Humanity is advancing towards the highest truth, the greatest happiness that it is possible to achieve on earth, and I am in the vanguard!"[46] Mr. Gorbachev replied that he was deeply touched.*

President Ikeda: Now, it is you, future division members, who are in the vanguard—as leaders of the twenty-first century!

Read books, engage with books, delve into books, and make friends with books! I hope you will go out into the world, challenging yourself in this way—with good books as your companions!

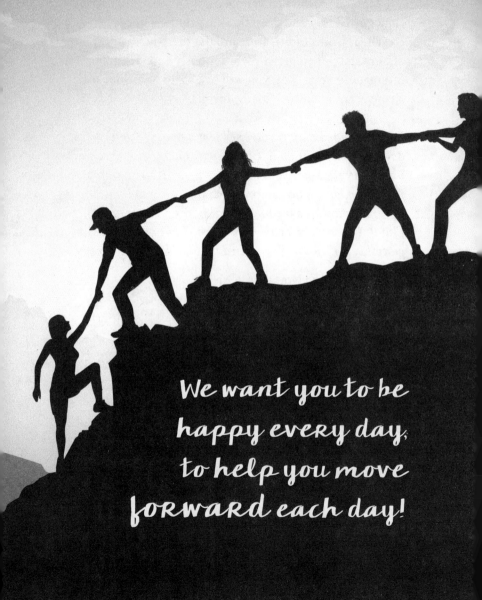

We want you to be
happy every day,
to help you move
forward each day!

Having Courage and
COMPASSION

Future Journal: *One member asks why SGI members can work so hard for others. She says she's amazed by her future division leader. "Although she's tired from working all day," she shares, "she still manages to have a bright smile when she comes to visit and encourage me."*

President Ikeda: This is a wonderful question. The member's gratitude and concern for her leader's well-being is a sign of her beautiful heart.

The SGI is solid thanks to all those who support our future division members. Their efforts arise from their sincerity. They want to hear about your struggles and chant with you. They want to know your personal goals and help you achieve them. They want you to be happy every day. They want to help you move forward each day. Their joy is seeing you do your best and seeing you grow and develop. You can take my word on that.

The sincere spirit to work for the happiness of others is what we refer to in Nichiren Buddhism as the world or life state of bodhisattva.

FJ: *Each person possesses the Ten Worlds—the worlds or life states of hell, hunger, animality, anger, humanity, heaven, learning, realization, bodhisattva, and Buddhahood. The ninth world is the world of bodhisattva. That's the life state of someone who seeks the correct teaching of Buddhism and is devoted to helping others become happy.*

Incidentally, the noted American scientist Dr. Linus Pauling, after hearing you give a speech in which you spoke about the Ten Worlds, said that he liked "number nine"— the world of bodhisattva—the best.[47]

President Ikeda: Yes, I remember that well.

When we chant Nam-myoho-renge-kyo, the world of bodhisattva emerges from within us. That is why SGI members can take action for others even when they are having a hard time themselves. By manifesting that pure, strong life state, they can encourage and inspire others.

Referring to the bodhisattva spirit, Nichiren writes: "[Bodhisattvas are those who think] little of their own lives but much of the lives of others. . . . [They hope] to bring salvation to all living beings and only after that to obtain Buddhahood" (WND-2, 201–202).

This perfectly describes our praiseworthy future division leaders. It is also the spirit of your parents who are SGI members. They devote their time and energy to offering encouragement, chanting, and taking action for the happiness of others. Even when they are criticized by those who misunderstand their intentions, they bravely forge ahead. The bodhisattva spirit has become their way of life. In a society in which people tend to care only about themselves, their work is incredibly noble. SGI members are true champions of sincerity.

The great Russian author Leo Tolstoy, whom I read avidly in my youth, wrote of his philosophy, "The only certain happiness in life is to live for others"[48] and "We live for ourselves only when we live for others."[49]

His words convey the essence of life. I would like to dedicate them to you. I think Tolstoy would have been delighted to meet all of you who are devoting your lives to the bodhisattva way.

"We live for ourselves only when we live for others."
—Leo Tolstoy

FJ: *Tolstoy was a great writer who loved humanity and did his utmost to help those who were less fortunate. His masterpiece* **War and Peace** *is treasured around the world.*

President Ikeda: Tolstoy lived the bodhisattva way. He established schools for peasant children. And when famine struck, he personally visited affected areas and set up relief centers to distribute food.

The starting point of Tolstoy's devotion to the people

was when he was just a boy. He lost his mother before his second birthday, and his father died when he was nine. He was then looked after lovingly by a distant relative, Tatyana Alexandrovna Ergolskaya. He once dedicated a poem to her thanking her for all that she had done for him. I believe that her sincere spirit to work for others became the foundation for Tolstoy's lifelong work.

FJ: We should never forget to repay the kindnesses shown to us. Along these lines, another member asks if working for others means that we must sacrifice ourselves.

President Ikeda: That is an important question.

Thinking only about oneself can lead to selfishness. Thinking only about others can lead to self-sacrifice. The point is to avoid either extreme. Rather, we can strive so that all of us—both ourselves and others—can enjoy life, grow, and become happy together. This is the source of true joy. The Daishonin says, "'Joy' means that oneself and others together experience joy" (OTT, 146).

Working for others means helping others find happiness. When those around us are happy, so are we. We feel a sense of purpose, meaning, and fulfillment. It brings us a joy that is far deeper and richer than that we can experience when merely striving for our own happiness.

"True happiness is not built on the misfortune of others"—these are words I once shared with Kansai Soka Schools students. Everyone enjoying happiness together; both ourselves and others filled with joy and wishing each other the best—this is the true purpose of life.

Nichiren writes, "If one lights a [lantern] for others, one will brighten one's own way" (WND-2, 1060). The actions we take for others' happiness lead to our own happiness as well. Above all, they cause our lives to shine. To live with altruism means to have the strength and wisdom to cherish both ourselves and others. The SGI is spreading this perspective of happiness throughout society and the world.

happiness

FJ: *Some say they have their hands full dealing with their own problems right now. They wonder if they'll be able to become people who can think about others' happiness.*

President Ikeda: Of course, the most important thing for you at this time is to train and develop yourselves. There is no need to go beyond what you can do now. That said, however, I hope you will try to do whatever you can, within your own limits, where you are right now.

Everyone has the world of bodhisattva, and it emerges in response to various external causes. For example, when you see an elderly person carrying a heavy bag or a friend struggling with a problem, you feel moved to help. That urge comes from the world of bodhisattva in your life. If you bring out just a little more courage than usual, you'll be able to be more considerate and take compassionate action for others.

President Toda said, "As ordinary mortals, it can sometimes be difficult for us to summon forth compassion, but we can substitute courage for compassion."

Chanting Nam-myoho-renge-kyo is the key that unlocks our courage. It enables us to bring forth the world of bodhisattva within us, irrespective of time, place, or circumstances.

FJ: *Recently, one of our high school division members in Fukushima Prefecture was part of a robotics team that won first place in the national preliminaries. In June [2013], they took second in a world contest, competing against college students from around the globe.*

They had built a robot to be used to help bring a nuclear accident under control.

President Ikeda: That is wonderful! Congratulations to them! I'm so happy to hear this!

Our lives begin to shine when we resolve to be of service to others. When you have the courage to do so, that courage transforms into compassion, and from compassion, wisdom is born.

The renowned American economist Dr. John Kenneth Galbraith once told me that consideration for others is the most important motivating force.

Those dedicated to working for the welfare of others may at times appear to be losing out because of all the effort involved. But the fact is that they are accumulating vast "treasures of the heart." Without a doubt, they will enjoy lives of absolute happiness and victory.

In the aftermath of the March 11 earthquake and tsunami in 2011, our fellow members in Tohoku have demonstrated the nobility and honor of working for others. We will never forget their example.

FJ: *Many have written saying that they want to work in a field where they can contribute to humanity or to help their friends who are struggling. Others have said that the idea of working for others seems vague, and they ask what concrete steps they can take.*

President Ikeda: To be thinking about what you can do for others is itself a wonderful first step to a great life.

As Buddhists, the first thing we can do is chant Nam-myoho-renge-kyo for our friends. Then, with the courage and compassion that arise as a result, we can reach out to them.

Think about what you can do in your daily life. For example, you might try talking to a classmate who looks lonely or try smiling and greeting someone who looks sad.

There are many ways to encourage those who are feeling down. Simply telling them that everything is going to be all right can lift their spirits. Even giving someone moral support can be a great comfort. These may seem like small gestures, but your sincerity can really encourage another person.

I hope that you will do your best to spread wonderful flowers of happiness, dialogue, and joy—in your homes, schools, communities, and throughout the world. Please become the mainstays of society, people on whom others can rely. This is my eternal prayer.

Spread wonderful flowers of happiness, dialogue, and joy!

Sowing the Seeds
of PEACE

Future Journal: *This summer, Soka Family Gatherings are being held throughout Japan with future division members taking part in the planning and operations.*

President Ikeda: That's great to hear. I'm excited at the thought of these wonderful gatherings. I'd like to thank the members of the future division for all your hard work. I hope the meetings will be meaningful and enjoyable, and that you will take care in the summer heat and be safe.

I would also like to thank everyone who is supporting the future division behind the scenes.

FJ: *Members in some areas are including presentations about peace.*

President Ikeda: That's an important topic. Nothing is more inspiring than seeing the baton of peace being carried on into the future.

Both the Soka Gakkai's first and second presidents were imprisoned for their opposition to the Japanese militarist authorities, who were driving the country to war. President Makiguchi died in prison for his beliefs. How happy both he and Mr. Toda would be to see your efforts!

FJ: *Your novel* **The Human Revolution** *opens with the lines "Nothing is more barbarous than war. Nothing is more cruel."*[50]

Future division members who have read this passage have asked to hear about your wartime experience.

President Ikeda: This question from young readers is extremely important, and it is my duty as the book's author to respond thoroughly.

On August 15, 1945, the day that World War II ended in Japan, I was seventeen—the same age as many of today's high school students. The war robbed us of our youth.

My family lived in what is now Ota Ward in Tokyo, and we made our living producing edible seaweed. My four older brothers, all in the prime of their youth, were drafted into the Japanese army. My father suffered from crippling rheumatism, which hurt the family business. My mother never complained, but I know it was very hard for her.

I had younger siblings, too, so I helped out with the seaweed production and took a job as a paperboy to earn some extra money.

When I graduated from the equivalent of today's junior high school, I began to work at a steel factory. I was fourteen. I wanted to continue my studies, but that wasn't possible. One of the cruel things about war is that it deprives young people of the opportunity to study.

In addition, I contracted tuberculosis. But since it was

wartime, I couldn't receive the treatment I needed, and I suffered terribly.

In 1938, as war approached, my parents had to sell the house they built. It later became part of a munitions factory. We moved to another house, but toward the end of the war, as air raids intensified, we were forced to evacuate it so that it could be torn down as part of a firebreak. Then, my family relocated to another part of Ota Ward, where we built a small house on land owned by a relative. The night before we were scheduled to move in, however, it was hit in a bombing raid and burned to the ground. We lost nearly everything. My brother and I managed to save a wooden chest, which contained my little sister's Girls' Day dolls.

While everyone else was disheartened by this terrible setback, my mother remained cheerful. "Someday we'll live in a fine house again where we can display these dolls properly," she said.

Mothers are amazing. With that single utterance, she rekindled hope in all our hearts.

FJ: *How did you feel when the war ended?*

President Ikeda: My first thought was "How quiet peace is!" We no longer had to worry about air-raid sirens going off or be frightened by the sound of exploding bombs.

I also thought, "How bright it is!" During the war, we were under blackout orders at night. It was dark both in our homes and on the streets. The day the war ended, as my mother prepared dinner, she said happily: "It's so bright. Now we can keep the lights on. How bright everything is!"

My father and mother both waited eagerly for the return of my brothers from the war. The following year, my brothers returned home one after another, all except the eldest.

In May 1947, almost two years after the war ended, the news finally arrived that my eldest brother had died in the fighting. He was my favorite brother. I have never been able to forget the sight of my mother. Her back was turned to us and her shoulders shook as she sobbed at the dreadful news.

> I do not believe in war as a means for creating peace.

All that war brings is tragedy. I do not believe in war as a means for creating peace. Even when war ends, the hellish suffering it has caused lives on. Not only my family but countless families throughout Japan experienced such suffering. That was true throughout Asia and other parts of the world too.

That's why war is an absolute evil. I hate war with every fiber of my being.

As a youth, I vowed to fight against the diabolical tendencies inherent in life that give rise to war.

FJ: *And then you met your mentor, Mr. Toda.*

President Ikeda: Yes. It was on August 14, 1947, a hot summer night, three months after learning of my eldest brother's death.

Japanese society was in a state of extreme confusion. I was nineteen and earnestly seeking the right way to lead my life. It was then that, together with friends, I went to a Soka Gakkai discussion meeting and saw a man with thick glasses talking to a group of about twenty people. "I want to eliminate all misery and suffering from the earth!" he said that night. His impassioned voice resounded through the room.

Mr. Toda was lecturing on Nichiren Daishonin's treatise "On Establishing the Correct Teaching for the Peace of the Land." This work teaches that in order to bring peace to the world, each individual must act based on a correct philosophy.

After his lecture finished, I asked him, "What is the correct way of life?"

He replied with warmth and familiarity, as if he had known me for a long time. Then, he said: "Try practicing Nichiren Buddhism. You are young. If you do so, the time will come, perhaps without you even being aware of it, when you will find yourself following the correct path through life."

I didn't grasp the profound teachings of Buddhism at the time, but I felt intuitively that I could completely trust Mr. Toda. Ten days later, on August 24—a hot Sunday as I recall—I joined the Soka Gakkai and began my journey on the path of mentor and disciple.

Sixty-six years [as of 2013] have passed since then. Following Mr. Toda's teachings, I have waged a struggle for peace through dialogue and have sown the seeds of peace around the world.

FJ: *Some members say that achieving peace sounds like such a big undertaking and they don't know where to start.*

President Ikeda: Just asking yourself honestly about the meaning of peace is a start. Even if you don't know what to do right now, just continuing to think about how to realize it will create ripples of peace.

The essence of war is violence. Violence exists in countless visible and invisible forms—from wars between countries and peoples to bullying at school or in society. When you see bullying at school and try to stop it, you are already building peace. It all begins from mustering your own courage.

While it's important to think about peace in terms of politics, diplomacy, and economics, people are what are behind all these areas. Peace can only be created by people.

Develop a
commitment
to PEACE...

The surest and soundest way to realize peace is for each of us to develop a commitment to peace.

FJ: *Another member asks simply, "Why do wars occur?"*

President Ikeda: Nichiren Daishonin writes, "Because anger increases in intensity, strife of arms occurs" (OTT, 33). In other words, anger driven by egoism is the root cause of war.

Anger is one of the three poisons, along with greed and foolishness. When that poison spreads, it causes unrest in society and leads to unending strife and war.

The world of Buddhahood is a strong, positive life state that seeks to guide everyone toward peace and happiness. To believe in the goodness of human beings and create hope out of every situation is the essence of Buddhahood. It is a life state of never giving up.

Nichiren Buddhism teaches that this state of life exists in all human beings.

Since we all have this infinitely noble life state, we need to value and care for our own lives as well as those of others. This is how we will bring an end to war. This is true for everyone, no matter their nationality or ethnic background.

We aim to make the philosophy of respect for the dignity of life the pervading spirit of the world. This is what is meant by "establishing the correct teaching for the peace of the land" in the modern age.

When we chant Nam-myoho-renge-kyo, the life state of Buddhahood emerges powerfully from within. Armed with courage, hope, and wisdom, we can illuminate everyone we encounter with the warm light of encouragement. Together, we can awaken to the fact that we all have that highest state of life inside us. We, SGI members, as noble Bodhisattvas of the Earth, talk with others to create a truly peaceful world for the sake of our friends, our communities, and society.

Peace is a constant struggle to transform despair into hope. It is the resolve to never lose faith in people. It is a song of praise to humanity, a song of the highest respect for our own lives and the lives of all others.

I'd like to share with you the words of Dr. Linus Pauling, who was a dear friend and a great scientist: "I believe that there is a greater power in the world than the evil power of military force, of nuclear bombs—there is the power of *good*, of *morality*, of *humanitarianism*. I believe in the power of the human spirit."[51]

FJ: *You published a dialogue with Dr. Pauling, who is considered one of the world's greatest scientists, on a par with Newton, Darwin, and Einstein. He was also a renowned peace activist.*

In his commentary following one of your lectures, he declared that the SGI was a great source of hope for the world.

President Ikeda: Dr. Pauling believed in the SGI and hoped we would carry on his work for peace. I met him four times, during which we talked about the future of humanity.

He was staunchly opposed to nuclear weapons. As a result, he was persecuted by his government, which was developing a nuclear program. Nevertheless, he was committed to speaking out against anything that would cause people to suffer. He wrote many articles and gave many speeches, persistently showing the way to peace.

Why was he able to continue his efforts despite the obstacles and persecution?

Let's take a look at his background. He was a sickly child and his family was poor. His father died when

Dr. Pauling was just nine. He worked part time while attending school to help out the family. Even after entering college, he continued to send money home.

Dr. Pauling's struggles in his youth taught him that we can accomplish whatever we set our minds to.

In his later years, he continued to speak out boldly and courageously for peace, without giving in to pressure by opponents.

His wife also supported him in every possible way. She was his comrade in the struggle for peace. Having a comrade—a friend you can trust from the depths of your heart who joins you in your struggle— is another important driving force for peace.

We have such like-minded friends, our

Linus and Ava Pauling

fellow SGI members, working alongside us all around the world. And most importantly, we have you, the future division members, to whom we will pass the baton of peace. This is my greatest pride and joy.

PEACE Starts Where You Are

Future Journal: *Many of those who read the previous installment sent in their determinations. One wrote: "I was reminded again that war never brings happiness, only misery. I am determined to work for peace by first valuing my own life and the lives of others—something that is very basic, yet most important."*

President Ikeda: That's wonderful. I am certain that because of all of you, the world will become a better place.

The flame of peace burns in your sincere determinations. The future of humanity is reflected in your earnest prayers. All of you, from such a young age, are practicing Nichiren Buddhism, a teaching of respect for the dignity of life. You are also studying hard so that you can contribute to peace. You are truly the hope of the world.

FJ: *Another person wrote: "Learning about the life of Dr. Linus Pauling, I was outraged by the persecution he had to endure as a peace activist. The same thing happened to President*

Ikeda. I wondered how he was able to continue his efforts for peace amid constant attack and opposition."

President Ikeda: That feeling of outrage is what we call "righteous anger." Nichiren writes, "Anger can be either a good or a bad thing" (WND-2, 931). In the last chapter, I quoted Nichiren where he said that anger driven by egoism is a cause of war. While that kind of anger certainly does exist, there is also a positive kind of anger, Nichiren tells us.

This is the righteous anger directed against the devilish nature that seeks to harm life, the greatest and most precious treasure of all. Such anger can generate constructive efforts for peace.

President Toda was angered by all injustice and inhumanity. And he felt a bitter fury for the wartime militarism that had caused his great and honorable mentor, Tsunesaburo Makiguchi, to die in prison.

This righteous anger is also evident in Mr. Toda's Declaration for the Abolition of Nuclear Weapons, which has become the proud starting point of our activities for peace. It was on September 8, 1957, at a youth division sports meet held in Kanagawa that Mr. Toda issued his immortal declaration: "We, the citizens of the world, have an inviolable right to live. Anyone who tries to jeopardize this right is a devil incarnate, a fiend, a monster."

He clearly perceived that war and nuclear weapons reflect the devilish nature in the depths of human beings. So he poured his whole life into this declaration out of a wish to conquer that devilish nature and protect people's lives. And he entrusted the youth with the great mission of

"We, the citizens of the world, have an inviolable right to live..."
—Josei Toda

spreading the idea that those who employ nuclear weapons should be viewed as "evil incarnate."

FJ: *The Pugwash Conferences on Science and World Affairs is an important association of scientists dedicated to the elimination of nuclear weapons.[52] One of its founders, Dr. Joseph Rotblat, called Mr. Toda "a heroic peace advocate and a martyr for peace."[53] In your dialogue with Dr. Rotblat, he also said: "Humankind is trapped in an extremely difficult predicament. Somehow, we must overcome this situation as soon as possible. I would like to ask you [President Ikeda] to exercise your global leadership to bring about a change in the situation necessary to ensure peace in the world."[54]*

President Ikeda: Dr. Rotblat was a great scientist and, along with Dr. Pauling, a signatory of the Russell-Einstein Manifesto [an appeal calling for the eradication of nuclear weapons and an end to war, signed by eleven world-renowned nuclear physicists in 1955]. Part of the manifesto reads, "We appeal as human beings to human beings:

Remember your humanity, and forget the rest."[55] This declaration, focusing on our shared humanity, resonates with the spirit of Mr. Toda's Declaration for the Abolition of Nuclear Weapons.

Lasting peace cannot be built through government policies and laws only. The basis for everything, first and foremost, is erecting a castle of peace in the hearts of human beings.

Mr. Toda was a great leader who loved the people. He was a lion for peace who stood up to eradicate misery from the world. He was a fierce warrior of truth and justice. That's why he wholeheartedly encouraged others and taught them of their important mission for peace. The day I heard President Toda's declaration, I was electrified. I resolved, as his disciple, to spend the rest of my life spreading his message throughout the world.

Since then, I have traveled the globe engaging in dialogue to bring humanity closer together. I have spoken with leaders of many nations. I have promoted exhibitions that convey the barbarity and ongoing threat of nuclear weapons. To build a world of peace and happiness, and to communicate my mentor's spirit, I have continued to take action, not intimidated by groundless criticism and attacks.

When we sail out into the ocean, we will be tossed by waves. When we climb a mountain, we will be buffeted by winds. Similarly, when we strive to do what's right, it's only natural that we will encounter opposition. I was fully aware of this fact. But I was determined, nevertheless, to spend my life fulfilling the vow I had made to my mentor.

FJ: *The SGI was established on January 26, 1975. Representatives from fifty-one nations and territories had gathered for the inaugural meeting. You said to them: "Rather than seeking after your own praise or glory, I hope that you will dedicate your noble lives to sowing the seeds of peace of the Mystic Law throughout the entire world. I shall do the same."*

President Ikeda: Now those seeds of peace have begun to blossom in 192 countries and territories. It is you, our future division members, who will ensure an even more brilliant flowering of peace.

Seeds are tiny. They aren't showy. They don't attract attention. But they patiently endure the heat of summer and the cold of winter, waiting for their moment to sprout and finally send forth beautiful blossoms. The same is true of our efforts for peace.

In that regard, I would like to share these words of my friend Dr. Elise Boulding, known for her advocacy of a culture of peace: "Peace is not only about acting in times of danger, it is also about assisting one another in daily life. The family and local community are key starting points."[56]

FJ: *Dr. Boulding has served as the president of the International Peace Research Association Foundation and a member of the U.N. University Council in Tokyo. She fought* *earnestly for peace even during World War II. She raised five children and dedicated her life to promoting peace. You and she published your dialogue under the title **Into Full Flower: Making Peace Cultures Happen**.*

President Ikeda: Yes, in that book, Dr. Boulding shared that her mother had a special influence on her life. As a young girl, she remembered her mother always being kind and considerate to the elderly people who lived in a care home nearby. Her mother sometimes took her there and encouraged her to sing and dance for them. She said her mother taught her that it is our responsibility to help make people happy.[57]

Actions for peace do not need to take place in some special arena. There are opportunities to work for peace in your homes, your schools, and your neighborhoods.

The fact is, wherever you are is your main arena for realizing peace. Your daily lives are the soil from which the seeds of peace will sprout and blossom.

"If there is going to be a peaceful world, we have to make it ourselves."
— Elise Boulding

FJ: *Many future division members have expressed*

their determination to do what they can where they are now. For instance, one writes: "I think seeking peace is something that anyone can do anywhere in the world. As one of those people, I will pray for peace and do whatever I can, in my own small way, to achieve it." And another says, "I may not be able to do much right now, but I will chant a lot, pray for world peace, and greet others cheerfully and make them smile."

President Ikeda: That's wonderful. And what you can do right here and now is definitely not insignificant. In fact, because you are in the precious period of your youth, you can do a lot to directly contribute to peace. Why? Because making friends is the driving force for peace. Being good to your parents is the wellspring of peace. And applying yourselves to your studies is the light of peace.

To the extent you and your friends encourage and support one another, as you develop good friendships, you are advancing peace. By growing into a fine individual and making your parents proud, you are spreading peace. And by studying hard and learning how to help and support others, you will be able to brighten the world with the light of peace.

Most importantly, by chanting Nam-myoho-renge-kyo, you can draw forth the infinite power and energy that lies hidden inside you.

Mahatma Gandhi, the father of Indian independence, believed that the power of the spirit is greater than the power of the atom bomb. The power within you is immeasurable, beyond the calculation of scientific equations such as Einstein's famous $E=mc^2$.

That's why I would like you to dedicate yourselves to chanting and cherishing those around you. Study hard, train yourselves mentally and physically, and grow into fine young adults. All of the efforts you make toward that end will become the seeds of peace.

FJ: *Many members said they were deeply moved to learn how cheerful and positive your mother was even when your house was burned to the ground. One member wrote: "I felt a profound feeling of respect for my own mother, who always tries to be cheerful for the rest of the family, no matter what's happening. I will continue to support and encourage her."*

President Ikeda: That beautiful feeling of respect for one's mother is a starting point for peace. The Daishonin says that he launched his great struggle to help all people attain enlightenment in order to repay the kindness of his mother (see WND-1, 931).

Dr. Boulding once attended a Soka Gakkai women's meeting in Japan. Sharing her impressions of our women's division members—the mothers of kosen-rufu—she said she could feel their genuine humanity and family-like warmth.

Mothers are great. They are strong, resilient, and gentle. If humanity could always remember the spirit of a mother's love, there would be no more wars.

When you cherish your mothers, you are cultivating the spirit of peace.

Please continue to strive and grow for the sake of your mothers. I hope you'll help her with the housework sometimes. At first, your mother may wonder what's going on. But just explain that you're taking your first step toward building peace! Your mother will be delighted to think that you're an emissary of peace.

And try to be nice to your father too!

FJ: *Two decades ago, on August 6, 1993, you began to write* **The New Human Revolution**. *August 6 is also the anniversary of the atomic bombing of Hiroshima in 1945.*

The novel starts with the words "Nothing is more precious than peace. Nothing brings more happiness. Peace is the most basic starting point for the advancement of humankind."[58] *Monuments engraved with those words have been erected in a number of places including Atsuta, Mr. Toda's hometown in Hokkaido; Hawaii, where you took your first step in your journey for world peace; and Guam, where the SGI was founded.*

President Ikeda: The twentieth century was a century of war. We need to ensure that the twenty-first century becomes a century of peace and respect for the dignity of life. I will continue to work, speak, and write toward that end.

Above all, I have you, my successors in the future division, who I believe are the greatest hope for the twenty-first century.

Take a courageous step forward and change the world! Become "torchbearers of justice," building and spreading peace! Demonstrate again today the boundless and invincible power of youth!

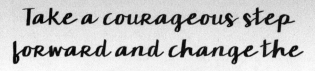

Take a courageous step forward and change the WORLD!

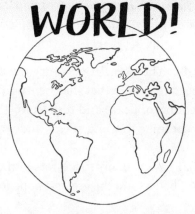

18

Seeking Inspiration That Enriches the HEART

Future Journal: *Tokyo has been selected as the venue for the 2020 Olympics and Paralympics. That is only seven years away [as of 2013]. Many who will compete in the 2020 games are now around the age of our future division members.*

President Ikeda: That's an exciting prospect!

The youthful leaders of kosen-rufu who visited Japan from sixty countries and territories last month [in September 2013] truly enjoyed meeting with future division members here.

Your vibrant growth is a source of tremendous hope for the entire world.

FJ: *Many in the future division are making this autumn a* *season of fresh challenges: studying, reading, playing sports, learning about the arts, and trying to do nice things for their parents.*

"EFFORT is the supreme joy."
—Pierre de Coubertin

President Ikeda: Autumn is the season of harvest, when the rice fields shimmer with gold. Pierre de Coubertin, founder of the modern Olympic Games, declared: "Effort is the supreme joy."[59] I hope that you will all work your hardest in your own way to make this a wonderfully fruitful autumn. Take time, too, to relax and gaze up at the clear blue sky.

FJ: *In talking with future division members, one gets the impression that many of them are extremely busy. Some say that they have so many things to do that it makes their heads spin.*

President Ikeda: I can well imagine. You go to school, do your classwork, play sports, do other activities, and then go home to study and do your homework. Some of you probably also attend after-school programs or take music or some other kind of lessons as well. And then, of course, there are your future division activities.

I am sure you are all doing your absolute best. That's very admirable. Please know that I praise you wholeheartedly, even if no one else may do so.

Having so many things to do can be very hard. But it's at such times that young people can really develop. Having nothing to do and just lazing about may be fun from time to time. But if every day is like that, you will get bored and won't feel any sense of accomplishment.

Not only people but all living things are constantly evolving and growing. Life never stands still for a moment. To be busy is to be alive. Finding ways amid your full schedules to encourage and motivate yourselves and to make progress each day are the keys to success in life.

Because you are so busy, please use your time wisely. Be sure to get enough sleep. You can't keep going very long without sleep. Make your health your top priority and don't overexert yourselves.

FJ: *We often hear we should control our time rather than be controlled by it. If we're stressed out, though, it's easy to feel pressured.*

President Ikeda: Yes, that's why a strong life force is so important. And we can gain that kind of life force from chanting.

Nichiren writes, "It is the power of the Buddhist Law that enables the deities of the sun and moon to make their rounds of the four continents" (WND-1, 685). The Mystic Law is the power underlying the unceasing workings of the universe. By chanting Nam-myoho-renge-kyo, we can cause our lives to brim with that infinite power.

If you've got a busy morning, it's all right to just chant Nam-myoho-renge-kyo three times to the Gohonzon. Chanting sincerely and strongly is what matters. Remember, you have at your disposal the most powerful tool of chanting. So even when you're busy, don't forget to chant. It will let you greet the day filled with life force as

vibrant and dynamic as the rising sun.

FJ: *Some members have asked about what they can do to stay happy and inspired when they're busy.*

President Ikeda: When you are striving to improve yourselves, your life is open to absorbing all kinds of things. You can derive that much more meaning from everything you encounter.

That is why, precisely because you are busy, I hope you will take every opportunity to expose yourself to positive things, things of beauty. You will be inspired. That emotion will then serve as spiritual nourishment, enriching your hearts and minds.

I founded the Tokyo Fuji Art Museum next to Soka University thirty years ago [in 1983] because I wanted the students and other young people to experience fine works of art.

President Toda often urged young people to seek out the finest in literature, music, and art. He trained and instructed us in many ways so that we would develop into outstanding citizens and cultured leaders of the people. He sometimes even took us to nice restaurants and taught us proper table manners.

Special training groups of the young men's and young women's divisions, such as the Suiko-kai and Kayo-kai, studied the classics of world literature under Mr. Toda. We learned about leadership, philosophy, and history in depth.

The books of Victor Hugo were among those the groups studied. Mr. Toda often urged us to read the great French author's works.

FJ: *Les Misérables is one of his most famous works. It has been made into a musical and film, and future division choruses have given stirring performances of some of the songs.*

President Ikeda: I was about fourteen or fifteen when I first read **Les Misérables**. I have since read it many times.

There is a bronze statue of Hugo at Soka University, depicting him striding forward. A famous passage from *Les Misérables* is engraved on the statue's base:

"There is one spectacle greater than the sea: That is the sky, there is one spectacle greater than the sky: That is the interior of the soul."[60]

I would like to dedicate these words of Hugo to you, the future division members. Your own hearts have the power to manifest potential even vaster than the sea or the sky.

FJ: *Hugo was a literary champion who brightened the hearts of the people in the turbulent nineteenth century. He carried on his courageous struggle, never discouraged by persecution at the hands of the authorities.*

President Ikeda: Hugo was physically weak as a child. His life was unsettled, and he had to move numerous times. Nevertheless, Hugo's mother encouraged him and his brothers to read many books. Reading became an enormous source of strength for Hugo.

He also learned a great deal from an elderly tutor who taught him Latin and Greek. Later, Hugo cited his mother, this elderly tutor, and the beautiful garden of his home, or nature, as the three teachers of his childhood.[61]

When Hugo was nine, he traveled to Spain. There he was deeply moved by the architecture and sculptures he saw, which awakened him to the power of art.

Encounters with outstanding individuals, good books, and the beauty of nature and art all cultivated and enriched Hugo's spirit. That spirit then poured forth from his pen to create great literature that overflows with love for the people.

It is very important to experience fine art and literature and meet outstanding individuals when you are young, as Hugo did. Your being moved and inspired will in turn enable you to inspire and bring joy to others.

FJ: *Reading the diaries from your youth,[62] we can see how, even amid your struggles and busy schedule, you still made time to enjoy music, literature, and art.*

President Ikeda: I did my utmost to follow Mr. Toda's guidance to seek out great works and outstanding individuals. At the same time, I was engaged in a real struggle each day to support Mr. Toda's businesses.

In my tiny apartment, I often listened to classical music. When I played Beethoven's Fifth Symphony or Ninth Symphony, my cramped apartment was transformed into a palace. When my fellow members came by, we would listen to the overture to Franz von Suppé's *Light Cavalry* and feel inspired.

Because our free time was so limited, just listening to a single piece of great music, reading a bit of great literature, or viewing a beautiful painting made a deep impression on our young lives.

But for me, the supreme examples of interacting with the best were my dialogues with Mr. Toda. He was a genius and a brilliant scholar, an unparalleled educator who truly loved young people. He was a fearless champion with strong convictions and a compassionate leader who valued the contributions of women. My greatest honor in life is to have been trained by such a mentor.

FJ: *Some students have said that although they try to be compassionate and generous, they remain focused on themselves. They find it difficult to be kind to their parents and friends, and they feel they are letting themselves down.*

President Ikeda: Please don't worry. Everyone goes through that. That's why we chant and make efforts to do our human revolution.

Being able to chant Nam-myoho-renge-kyo is truly amazing. You can chant for your own happiness, and you can chant for those around you, including your parents, siblings, and friends.

What does it mean to have a big heart? It is how much you can care for another person and how much you can extend your concern to those around you. The more deeply you chant for your friends and others, the bigger your heart becomes.

I have found such expansive hearts in the outstanding individuals that I have met around the world. People who care about world peace and take action for the welfare of humanity have hearts big enough to embrace the world. They are friends with all human beings.

A Buddhist sutra teaches that "the mind is like a skilled painter" (WND-1, 226). Like a skilled painter, our minds can depict anything.

As young people who embrace the Mystic Law, you are brilliant painters of hope, great artists of creating happiness. Whatever you can imagine, you can achieve. Once you have awakened to this power of your mind, you can create tremendous value each day and build a magnificent future.

> Whatever you can imagine, you can achieve.

FJ: *Many world leaders have said how impressed they are that SGI members around the world are awakening to their*

missions, demonstrating their abilities to the fullest, and
striving as good citizens.

President Ikeda: The examples of human revolution
achieved by SGI members, including your families, are a
model for people all around the world.

I would also like all of you to try your hardest to
realize your dreams. When you undertake this challenge,
you will come to experience the infinite inner expanse and
greatness of your own lives.

Nichiren writes: "One may put [the mind] inside a
mustard seed and the mustard seed will not be stretched
nor will the mind be cramped thereby. One may put it in
the vast heavens and the heavens will not be too broad for
it nor the mind too narrow to fill them" (WND-2, 843).

No matter how confining your circumstances may
seem, you can have a big heart that nothing can tie down.
At the same time, when you go out into a vast, unknown
world, your mind can soar without bounds.

The mind is always free and unfettered; it has limitless
power. Faith in the Mystic Law draws out that great power.
Chanting Nam-myoho-renge-kyo lets us reveal our best
possible self. The reason we practice Nichiren Buddhism
is to unlock our potential, which is vaster than the sea or
the sky.

My young friends, become world
leaders with big hearts! Become experts
in the art of happiness who can embrace
others warmly with a rich spirit!

19

Envisioning a Hope-Filled Future TOGETHER

Future Journal: *The long-awaited new Soka Gakkai Headquarters building in Shinanomachi, Tokyo, has been completed at last [October 2013] and a new era of worldwide kosen-rufu has begun.*

President Ikeda: Yes. And the future division members will play the leading role in this new era.

This Hall of the Great Vow for Kosen-rufu is a shining castle for our future division members. You are the ones who will shoulder the future of Soka from now on, illuminating humanity with the light of hope.

FJ: *The handover of the new building took place on October 2, SGI World Peace Day. It was on this day in 1960 that you embarked on your travels for world peace. As you know, a beautiful rainbow appeared in the sky on the day of the handover.*

President Ikeda: Yes, no doubt the heavenly deities were celebrating with us! To me, the rainbow symbolized the bright future of all of you, our young members. It seemed to represent your proud mission of building rainbow bridges of peace and hope around the world.

In 2030, when the Soka Gakkai celebrates its one hundredth anniversary, I know that all of you will have grown into outstanding leaders of kosen-rufu. Some of you will have jobs that take you around the world. Some of you will be scholars researching new fields of learning. Some of you will be educators fostering capable young people. Some of you will be business leaders or entrepreneurs. Some of you will be physicians or nurses protecting human life. Some of you will be great artists or inspiring athletes. Some of you will be making wonderful contributions to people's welfare as leaders of your community or of society.

I look forward eagerly to your bright futures. I believe in you. I believe in you completely. I hope you will also believe in your abilities and your futures and strive to make your dreams come true. I am chanting seriously for all of your futures to open boundlessly and brilliantly before you.

> **Strive to make your dreams come true.**

FJ: *A cartoon envisaging the Soka Gakkai five decades in the future appeared in the January 1, 1969, edition of the* **Seikyo Shimbun.** *It contained some really imaginative futuristic visions, including a Soka school on Mars and an underwater Soka University campus!*

There were many other elements in the cartoon, however, that have already become a reality—such as live television broadcasts of headquarters leaders meetings, people the world over coming to Japan to discuss Buddhism, and international conferences using multilingual interpreting devices. It's impressive that these visions, which seemed like a dream at the time, have been realized under your leadership.

President Ikeda: Our society is developing faster and faster. Many things that seem impossible today will be commonplace fifty years from now. In fact, the things you imagine today can become the reality of the future, the future of kosen-rufu.

Nichiren quotes a sutra that says, "If you want to understand what results will be manifested in the future, look at the causes that exist in the present" (WND-1, 279). No matter what has happened until now, change is always possible. We can create a new path from the present into the future.

All of you have within your lives the power to calmly overcome whatever you are facing now. You just have to tap into that power. That's why, even if you experience disappointment, I want you to bring forth invincible courage and envision a better future. If you look toward the future, your horizons will expand. When you imagine a brighter future, you'll know what you need to do right now.

When I spoke with the African environmental activist Wangari Maathai, she said that young people "need to understand that there is no future—the future is now. If they want to see the future, they must act now."

I would like to dedicate those words, which epitomized Dr. Maathai's life, to all of you.

FJ: *Dr. Maathai was born in Kenya. Deeply troubled by the destruction of forests in her homeland, she founded the Green Belt Movement, an environmental nongovernmental organization that planted forty million trees throughout Africa. In 2004, Dr. Maathai was awarded the Nobel Peace Prize.*

President Ikeda: Yes, Dr. Maathai kindly lectured at Soka University. She had the highest hopes and expectations for the young people of the SGI.

Dr. Maathai was raised in a rural area at the foot of Mount Kenya. She earned a doctorate at the University of Nairobi, one of Africa's leading universities, and was the first woman to gain a faculty position there. She was a person of diligence and perseverance.

FJ: *Her efforts to protect the environment were met with prejudice and personal slander. She was arrested and imprisoned numerous times. Once she was actually beaten unconscious by those opposed to her activities.*

Wangari Maathai

President Ikeda: She was persecuted because her cause was just, because she was doing great things. But Dr. Maathai kept on with her struggle, refusing to be intimidated. No matter how hard things were, no matter what happened, she looked to the future and never let go of hope.

When she was in high school, she had wonderful teachers with whom she could talk freely and who supported her warmly. She remained in contact with them even after she graduated.

Because of that humanistic education, Dr. Maathai recalled, she could grow up with the belief that "a general orientation toward trusting people and a positive attitude toward life and fellow human beings is healthy."[63] She learned to find hope for the future, for her fellow human beings, and for society even in the most hopeless situations.

There is no need to dwell on the past or have regrets; no need to compare yourself unfavorably to others; no need to focus only on what you are unable to do. Instead of looking to the past, look to the future. Instead of being jealous of others and thinking about what you can't do, start from what you can do now, at your own pace.

Those who can fully use their abilities are the real winners in life. Even when everything seems hopeless, it's important to continue doing your best. Everyone has the ability to try. *The future is always filled with hope.*

It was to secure a bright future for the SGI that I established the high school and junior high school divisions—in 1964 and 1965, respectively. The high school division will celebrate its fiftieth anniversary next year [in 2014] and the junior high school division the year after [in 2015].

Nineteen sixty-four was the year that the Tokyo Olympics were held. That December, while visiting Okinawa, I began writing *The Human Revolution*.

When I established the high school division, some leaders expressed a contrary opinion. While it might be an important step for the future, they said, there were many other more pressing matters at hand. But I was adamant, telling them: "I am concerned about the Soka Gakkai thirty or forty years down the line. Today's high school students will be the leaders of our organization then." I have always believed that unless we foster the future division members, there would be no future for kosen-rufu.

I am happy to say that those early future division members have grown into capable leaders of kosen-rufu and society. They have worked together with me to build the Soka Gakkai into a strong organization. My feelings for today's future division members are exactly the same as they were fifty years ago.

In a way, the completion of the Hall of the Great Vow marks a fresh starting point on our journey to realize our shared dream of kosen-rufu. Let's make a fresh start together each day.

I want to look to the future and share dreams for the future together with you. I want to look on as you soar magnificently into the world from the Hall of the Great Vow. That is my vision for the future. To achieve that, I am determined to continue to open the way forward and do whatever I can to support you.

FJ: *A high school student has asked about the significance of November, the month of the Soka Gakkai's founding.*

President Ikeda: Wanting to learn about the Soka Gakkai is commendable.

On November 18, 1930, our founder, the educator Tsunesaburo Makiguchi, published the first volume of *The System of Value-Creating Education*. In it, he outlined his educational philosophy. In an age dominated by militarism, he proclaimed that the true aim of education was not the benefit of the nation but the happiness of children. The date of this work's publication marks the day of the Soka Gakkai's founding.

President Toda supported Mr. Makiguchi behind the scenes and made it possible for him to publish his book. Mr. Toda did everything he could to assist his mentor, from organizing Mr. Makiguchi's ideas and editing the manuscript to raising the money for publication.

The first editions of Tsunesaburo Makiguchi's *System of Value-Creating Education*.

In the middle of World War II, Mr. Makiguchi was arrested and imprisoned for refusing to compromise his beliefs and obey the orders of the militarist government to accept State Shinto. He continued to speak out for what he believed was right even while in prison. He eventually died there, on November 18, 1944. He lived a truly noble life, one dedicated to Nichiren Buddhism and the happiness of others.

Mr. Toda was imprisoned along with Mr. Makiguchi. On July 3, 1945, a short time before the war ended, he was released. Carrying on the vision of his mentor, he immediately set about rebuilding the Soka Gakkai.

When Mr. Makiguchi was imprisoned, one after another of his disciples denounced him and quit the Soka Gakkai. But Mr. Toda stayed true to his mentor. He declared his gratitude with the words "In your vast and boundless compassion, you let me accompany you even to prison."

I, too, followed that noble, solemn path of mentor and disciple selflessly dedicated to a shared ideal.

Nichiren writes, "The lion king fears no other beast, nor do its cubs" (WND-1, 997). Striving alongside one's mentor with fearless and unwavering commitment, no matter what happens, is the spirit and foundation of the mentors and disciples of Soka. This has been the source of the Soka Gakkai's growth and development until now, and it will continue to be so.

The Hall of the Great Vow for Kosen-rufu is a great citadel. There members will renew their vow to realize worldwide kosen-rufu, carrying on the spirit of mentor and disciple. I am sure that both Mr. Makiguchi and Mr. Toda are joyously watching over our future division members, who will make their departure into the future from this citadel.

FJ: *As future division leaders, we are determined to communicate the mentor-disciple spirit to our members during the month of the Soka Gakkai's founding.*

President Ikeda: I would like to thank all of our future division leaders. I cannot begin to fully express my gratitude for your efforts. The mentor-disciple spirit burning in your hearts will naturally be communicated to your members. It is passed from heart to heart, one soul harmonizing with another.

I know that even when you are busy with work or are tired, you go out to visit and encourage members. Your hearts brim with the Soka Gakkai spirit. While dealing with your own problems, you listen to the concerns of these young people and chant with them. There are no nobler efforts to foster capable individuals. Your efforts and prayers themselves overflow with the spirit of mentor and disciple. They cannot fail to touch the hearts of the young people you are supporting. You are always looking toward the future of the Soka Gakkai together with me, sharing my spirit.

November 18, Soka Gakkai Founding Day, will soon be here. It is none other than you, the members of the future division, who will carry on the baton of our founding spirit. I place my deepest trust in you, the protagonists of the new era of worldwide kosen-rufu. Each one of you represents the bright future of Soka.

20

Win With Nichiren's WRITINGS

Future Journal: *Many high school division members studied hard and took the Soka Gakkai Study Department entrance examination last month [November 2013].*

President Ikeda: I know you did your very best, in spite of being busy with school and other things. Your efforts are something to be proud of. That you tried to learn about the world's foremost life philosophy is itself an achievement.

Let's continue to chant, study, and practice together, taking to heart Nichiren's words "Exert yourself in the two ways of practice and study" (WND-1, 386). I look forward to each one of you becoming a victor in faith and an expert in peace and happiness.

I would also like to sincerely thank all the future division leaders and other seniors in faith who taught, encouraged, and supported the students for the study exam.

FJ: *At discussion meetings, many future division members are reading from our publications. One asks why we always study* *passages from Nichiren's writings at discussion meetings.*

President Ikeda: That's a very perceptive question! The SGI always moves forward based on Nichiren's writings. They contain a winning philosophy that enables us to open up our lives. They are a fountain of the highest wisdom, and they have the power to call forth indomitable courage from within us.

President Toda was a brilliant mathematician, a man of reason. He often said that faith seeks reason and reason deepens faith.

As you practice Nichiren Buddhism seriously, you may start to wonder why we chant and why our prayers are answered. You'll want to know the reasoning behind these things. Studying Nichiren's writings can provide you with the answers. At the same time, looking for those answers helps further deepen your faith.

Nichiren writes: "The [Chinese] characters of [the Lotus Sutra] are all without exception living Buddhas. . . . But because we have the eyes of ordinary people, we see them as characters" (WND-1, 486). If you continue to read Nichiren's writings, and regularly chant Nam-myoho-renge-kyo, all the words contained in the writings will come to display the power of the Buddha and be absorbed into your young lives.

In his writings, we can see Nichiren's firm resolve to uphold the correct teaching of Buddhism. We can see his powerful conviction that all forms of hardship and adversity can be overcome without fail. The Daishonin shows us the way to attain absolute happiness, so that life itself becomes an unsurpassed joy.

Studying his writings, therefore, enables you to become an invincible champion, a sun illuminating your friends with hope, and a person who can wisely lead the world to peace.

FJ: *Some say they find some of the writings difficult to understand.*

President Ikeda: I can relate to that. I remember writing in my diary as a young man: "Read the Gosho [Nichiren's writings]. It is extremely difficult"[64] and "Whenever I participate in a study meeting, I feel I have not studied enough. Profoundly aware of the importance of study."[65]

I gave my all to learning under Mr. Toda. On his behalf, I also lectured on the writings many times. No matter how tired I was when I got home at the end of the day, I made it a habit to read Nichiren's writings and record in my diary a passage that resonated with me.

Interestingly enough, you'll find that those passages you engrave in your life when you are young will always remain with you. Even if you don't fully understand them at first, their meaning will eventually become clear to you.

Today, SGI members around the world are eagerly studying Nichiren Buddhism.

Naturally, it's important to try to understand the principles of Buddhism intellectually. But even more crucial is engraving the Daishonin's writings in your heart and putting them into practice in your life.

Many of your parents do activities based on Nichiren's writings and bring the spirit of the Daishonin to life.

Many SGI members, for instance, when faced with difficulties, remembered the Daishonin's teaching "Employ the strategy of the Lotus Sutra before any other" (WND-1, 1001). Telling themselves not to strategize but to chant, they found the courage to surmount their problems.

When they felt demoralized and down on themselves, many members recalled the words "'Attain' means to open or reveal" (OTT, 126). They then went on to reveal their vast inner potential and achieve remarkable personal growth.

If you take to heart even one passage, earnestly chant, and continue to make steady efforts, your youth and your life will definitely open up. Engraving Nichiren's writings in your heart and putting them into practice will give you unshakable conviction in the power of faith and in your ability to win. The passage you choose as your inspiration will become your conviction and be reflected in the way you live your life. Those who have a favorite passage are strong. They are unbeatable when they face obstacles.

Engrave Nichiren's writings in your heart.

This is a good opportunity, so why not try asking your family or seniors in faith about their favorite passages? I'm sure they'll share them, and a related experience, with you.

FJ: *Those passages are a compass guiding each person's life.*

President Ikeda: I'll never forget what the writer Mikhail Sholokhov said to me on my first visit to Russia [in 1974]: "A person's convictions are what matter. They provide the power for attaining one's goals. You can't achieve anything without convictions." I would like to dedicate these words to you, my young friends.

Fame and social status are not what make a person great. Those who have noble convictions are great. And faith in the Mystic Law is the path of supreme conviction.

FJ: *Mikhail Sholokhov was a Nobel laureate in literature and one of the most influential Russian writers of the twentieth century. Among his best-known works are* **And Quiet Flows the Don** *and* **The Fate of a Man**.

President Ikeda: Sholokhov was a great writer who lived among the people and depicted the flowing river of history in his works. He was a champion who overcame adversity through his convictions.

He was born in an impoverished village in southern Russia. There was fierce fighting going on at the time as part of the Russian civil war. Because of that, he was unable to continue his formal schooling beyond age thirteen. After the war, at seventeen, he went to Moscow to resume his studies but was unable to enter school. Instead, he had to support himself through hard manual labor.

Still, he wasn't beaten. He studied on his own, wrote stories, and spoke about his ideals with like-minded friends. When he was eighteen, he published his first short story under a pseudonym and began his career as a writer.

The works of the great authors inspired his ambitions

and creativity. Amid his difficulties, he found encouragement and inspiration in the words of Tolstoy, Chekhov, Pushkin, Gorky, and Gogol.

To continue to study even amid the most challenging circumstances, to find hope, and to transform those difficulties into fuel for growth underscores my conviction that learning is light.

FJ: *One young man shares that he came from a poor family. His parents were always arguing from the time he was little. As a high school student, he became rebellious and spent all his time hanging out with friends.*

Then, when he was in his last year of high school, a future division leader visited his home. At first, he refused to see him, but the leader just kept coming back.

The leader shared with him the passage "Winter always turns to spring" (WND-1, 536), and a flame of hope was kindled in his heart.

After that, he began to practice Buddhism seriously. He has shown actual proof and turned his karma into a mission by using his experience to encourage his friends. Today, his family is harmonious, and he feels that the spring of happiness has indeed come.

President Ikeda: That's a wonderful story. The leader who refused to give up and continued to warmly encourage him is truly admirable.

Nichiren's writings are a beacon of hope that can

illuminate the darkest misery. The vibrant efforts of SGI members around the globe give testimony to this.

You will no doubt come up against all sorts of difficulties in your lives. At such times, you may wonder why this happens even though you are chanting or why your wishes do not come true.

That's when I would like you to read Nichiren's words. By studying his writings, you come into contact with the life of Nichiren Daishonin. You are bound to feel courage, wisdom, and hope well up from within.

Then with a renewed vow and earnest prayer, you can face your situation head-on.

FJ: *Some of our readers have asked about your favorite passages.*

President Ikeda: I have many. Among my favorites is one from **The Record of the Orally Transmitted Teachings** that I learned from Mr. Toda. He told me: "Engrave this in your heart! Champions must never forget it!"

> **If in a single moment of life we exhaust the pains and trials of millions of kalpas, then instant after instant there will arise in us the three Buddha bodies[66] with which we are eternally endowed. Nam-myoho-renge-kyo is just such a "diligent" practice. (OTT, 214)**

"The three Buddha bodies with which we are eternally endowed" means the life state of Buddhahood within us. To access and bring forth that life state at each moment, we must in that moment exert "the pains and trials of millions of kalpas," that is, an eternity. By chanting Nam-myoho-renge-kyo and striving for kosen-rufu, we summon forth the courage and wisdom to do just that.

This passage has supported me in every struggle I've faced. I have overcome everything and triumphed completely by chanting with an intensity to compress all eternity into a single moment of life.

I am also fond of a passage from "The Opening of the Eyes" that I have shared many times: "Although I and my disciples may encounter various difficulties, if we do not harbor doubts in our hearts, we will as a matter of course attain Buddhahood" (WND-1, 283).

It is because we uphold the correct teaching that we encounter difficulties. That's why if we keep pressing forward, don't let anything shake our conviction, and summon ever stronger faith, we can transform poison into medicine without fail.

"I and my disciples" refers to mentor and disciple. When mentor and disciple act based on a shared vow, there is no problem they cannot surmount. They will absolutely reach their lofty goal.

Basing our actions on this passage, we of the SGI have realized tremendous growth. The mentors and disciples of Soka have triumphed over all. And we will continue to achieve even greater victories.

A new era of worldwide kosen-rufu has arrived. I am chanting and waiting for you to take your places on the stage of world peace. I am chanting for you to play important roles there as the protagonists of the future, always upholding the supreme philosophy of life embodied in Nichiren's writings.

21

Take a COURAGEOUS
Step Toward the World Stage!

President Ikeda: The sun has risen on a hope-filled new year. Happy New Year to all future division members! I've been receiving many new year' determinations from future division members in Japan and around the world.

Future Journal: *This year [2014], the Year of Opening a New Era of Worldwide Kosen-rufu, is also the fiftieth anniversary of the future division. The future division members, the protagonists of the new era, are excited about the year ahead.*

President Ikeda: I am happy to hear that. Let's also make it a year of opening a new era of the future division!

President Toda had high hopes for our precious young successors. He once said: "In the future, we must build a peaceful world of global citizenship, free of national and ethnic division—a world in which anyone can experience true happiness. I hope you will remember what I've said here today and contribute to achieving this dream, even in a small way."

Mr. Toda treated the children he spoke to as adults, showing them the utmost respect. He passionately shared his grand vision of global citizenship with them.

He was convinced that young people who embraced the supreme teaching of Nichiren Buddhism were already world leaders. He believed that all young people have bright potential. He believed in them and taught them about the great mission of worldwide kosen-rufu.

Nichiren Buddhism teaches that those who take on the mission of kosen-rufu in this era are Bodhisattvas of the Earth. Do you know what Bodhisattvas of the Earth are? Some of you may have heard this term mentioned at discussion meetings or seen it on a study exam.

FJ: *The Bodhisattvas of the Earth are a vast multitude of beings who emerge from the earth during the assembly where the Lotus Sutra is taught. There they pledge to their teacher, Shakyamuni Buddha, to spread the correct teaching of Buddhism in his stead. They pledge to help all living beings become happy in the troubled age after the Buddha's passing.*

President Ikeda: Yes, in the sutra, each Bodhisattva of the Earth is described as emitting a golden light, just like the Buddha. They are all so magnificent that even the most remarkable followers of Shakyamuni were completely astonished.

According to the sutra, the Bodhisattvas of the Earth have vast wisdom, firm resolve, and a boundless spirit to seek the Buddhist teachings. They are masters of dialogue, inspiring to behold, and trustworthy. They are characterized as leaders committed to helping people become happy. When they appear in the assembly, they are accompanied by countless friends.

The stage on which the Bodhisattvas of the Earth carry out their mission is the real world. With courage, hope, and wisdom, they illuminate the hearts of those facing problems. The Bodhisattvas of the Earth also vow to their teacher to spread his teachings far and wide.

> With courage, hope, and wisdom, they *illuminate the hearts of those facing problems.*

So who are these incredibly noble and admirable Bodhisattvas of the Earth today? They are none other than the members of the SGI.

In our troubled world, there are negative people who try to obstruct those who work for a just and noble cause. The SGI alone, in spite of such obstacles, is making kosen-rufu a reality. The SGI is sharing Buddhism with others and helping them become happy.

The truth is, each one of you has been born into this world based on the vow you have made as a Bodhisattva of the Earth.

FJ: *Some may be thinking: "I couldn't be a Bodhisattva of* *the Earth. My grades aren't very good" or "I am not that accomplished."*

President Ikeda: You may feel that way now, but everyone who embraces this Buddhism is infinitely noble.

Nichiren Daishonin states: "Nichiren and his followers, who now chant Nam-myoho-renge-kyo, are all followers of these [leaders of] bodhisattvas who emerged from the earth" (see OTT, 118) and "Were they not Bodhisattvas of the Earth, they could not chant [Nam-myoho-renge-kyo]" (WND-1, 385).

You are all chanting Nam-myoho-renge-kyo and doing your best in a way that's true to yourselves. You practice along with the SGI, which is advancing worldwide kosen-rufu, the cherished wish of the Daishonin. That in itself is unmistakable proof that you are Bodhisattvas of the Earth.

Those who chant Nam-myoho-renge-kyo can tap into their boundless potential. They can draw forth inexhaustible wisdom from within. They can impart hope to others through their inspiring example of courage and confidence.

All of you have embraced the Mystic Law at such a young age. And you are challenging yourselves in your studies. The doors to the world are wide open before you. When you chant seriously and act for the welfare and happiness of others, then wherever you go, wherever it may be in the world, that will be the perfect place for you to shine.

At this significant time of opening a new era, all of you who are studying hard definitely have a great mission to fulfill as leaders on the world stage.

FJ: *One student asked: "One day, I want to travel around the world, meet all kinds of people, and share hopes and dreams with one another. What can I do now to prepare myself for that?"*

President Ikeda: That's a wonderful goal! The world is waiting for all of you. You are the hope of humanity.

There are many things you can do now to prepare for an active role on the world stage. For instance, you can work hard at school, learn foreign languages, read good books, and exercise both your bodies and minds.

But there is no need to rush. As the saying goes, "A journey of a thousand miles begins with a single step." The steps you take one after another right now will lead you to great future achievements.

I would like to share these words from the autobiography of former South African president Nelson Mandela, who died in December [2013] at age ninety-five: "I have discovered the secret that after climbing a great hill, one only finds that there are many more hills to climb."[67]

When you climb to the top of a hill, a grand new vista stretches out before you. There you will come to see even more hills to climb ahead. In life, all of these hills, or challenges, can be seen as "hills of your mission" that you and you alone must climb. Since that is the case, just climb the next hill. When you exert all your strength and reach the top, another new view will await you.

Youth is a time of taking on one challenge after another. Those who have the invincible spirit to keep striving are true victors in life.

Nelson Mandela and Daisaku Ikeda meet in Tokyo, October 1990.

FJ: *Nelson Mandela was a great man who fought tirelessly against apartheid—the notorious system of racial discrimination.*

He spent more than twenty-seven years in prison for his beliefs. After his release, he was elected the first black South African president and worked toward building a "rainbow nation" in which all people could live together in harmony.

President Ikeda: He was an indomitable champion of truth and justice. He was a fearless crusader for human rights whose compassion embraced everyone.

He endured more than ten thousand days in prison. Eight months after his release, he visited the Seikyo Shimbun Building in Shinanomachi, Tokyo. There I welcomed him together with many youth. I will never forget how bright his smile was.

From the day he was released, he immediately took action. He traveled all over South Africa and encouraged the people to work with him to create a society in which everyone could live harmoniously.

"I dare not linger," he wrote, "for my long walk is not yet ended."[68] He continued to advance on the road to freedom without rest. He kept on climbing the many "hills of mission" that continued to appear before him.

I hope that all of you, like President Mandela, will climb the hills before you, never giving up, with the resolve to never be defeated. If you do, I guarantee that you will come to see the summit of your dreams.

FJ: *The time of youth could be described as a series of struggles, with many "hills" of problems and challenges to be faced.*

President Ikeda: Yes, that's true. That's why it's important to take even one brave step forward.

When President Mandela was still a teenager, he etched in his heart the moral of a story he had heard: "*Don't* run away from your problems; *face* them! Because *if you don't deal* with them, they will *always* be with you. *Deal* with a problem which arises; face it courageously."[69] It was a lesson he never forgot.

Because he continued to win over his inner weaknesses and strengthen his courage, he could overcome all kinds of adversity, including discrimination, persecution, and many harsh years in prison. His long years of challenge and struggle are undoubtedly what made Nelson Mandela the great figure who is acclaimed by people all around the world today.

Courage does not mean being free of fear. True courage is not giving in to the fear we feel and, instead, continuing to challenge ourselves. A person with such courage can change the world.

> **TRUE COURAGE** is not giving in to the fear we feel and, instead, continuing to *challenge ourselves*.

FJ: *Another member asked specifically: "Someday I would like to work for world peace and the happiness of all people. To do that, should I try for an international career?"*

President Ikeda: I, of course, want you all to become capable people who play active roles in the world. But this does not necessarily mean that you have to go overseas or find some kind of international job.

Living out your life confidently in the place where you are right now is the foundation of worldwide kosen-rufu. There is no need for you to think that just because you've stayed in your own country you can't contribute to worldwide kosen-rufu.

Recently, I received some messages from SGI members who had been deeply moved by meeting future division members in Japan. They were surprised to learn that these young people were studying Nichiren's writings. They said that as soon as they returned home, they would do the same with future division members there. Your efforts can greatly influence the world.

The information age is advancing rapidly. The world is becoming smaller, more closely linked. For your generation, wherever you are and whatever your situation may be, the world is your stage. That's precisely why it's important to always uphold a noble aspiration, to be committed to contributing to worldwide kosen-rufu. Your prayers for that will not fail to be answered. For you were all born to bring smiles to people's faces and give them joy.

You have a great future ahead of you. You have unlimited potential. It is for you that I have continued to open new paths. I am entrusting you to achieve kosen-rufu in your respective countries and throughout the world.

You are the successors of our SGI movement. The new era of worldwide kosen-rufu is the brilliant age when you become deeply aware of your mission as Bodhisattvas of the Earth and grow into individuals who can impart hope and courage to people around the globe.

22

Nothing Is Greater Than the Path of MENTOR and DISCIPLE

President Ikeda: Nichiren Daishonin writes, "Winter always turns to spring" (WND-1, 536). SGI members around the world have cherished this passage while facing difficulties.

Precisely because winter can be harsh, we greet spring with boundless joy. I know that many young members in Japan are now applying themselves to preparing for school entrance examinations.[70]

President Toda, was born in the cold month of February [February 11, 1900]. He was a great educator. One winter day, a student of his was going to take a school entrance exam. He warmly encouraged this student outside the examination site, saying: "Relax and think carefully as you answer the questions. I know you'll do fine!" The student later said that he was deeply encouraged. He was able to put everything he had into the exam because he felt Mr. Toda was watching over him.

I am also earnestly chanting that all of you taking exams will do your best and blaze a new hope-filled path forward. Please take care of your health. Remember to eat well and get enough sleep. Have confidence and apply what you have learned from your hard work.

Future Journal: President Toda was born in 1900, which means that our present junior high school division members were born almost exactly a century after him.

President Ikeda: Mr. Toda was born at the start of the twentieth century and illuminated that century. You, the future division members, have emerged at the start of the twenty-first century and are going to light up this century.

More than any gift he could receive, Mr. Toda rejoiced in the growth of his disciples and reports of their victories. That's why, since my youth, I have always taken on a new challenge in February. I was determined to crown the month of his birth with the growth and victories of his disciples.

FJ: *Whenever you speak of President Toda, we are moved by how noble the path of mentor and disciple is. Future division members have asked if you can tell them more about the path of mentor and disciple and why it's important.*

President Ikeda: The path of mentor and disciple is not something unusual. Just as birds follow the path of birds, and fish follow the path of fish, human beings also have their paths. The path of mentor and disciple enables us to lead the most dignified and meaningful lives and to keep striving to improve ourselves.

In fields such as academia, the arts, and sports, too, there are mentors who teach the correct path. Mr. Toda is my mentor because he taught me the path of Buddhism and the correct way to live as a human being.

When the brutal conflict of World War II ended in 1945, I was seventeen—the same age as many high school students. Many adults who insisted that we should be willing to die for our country changed their tune overnight. They started to express new values and ways of thinking—speaking of peace, freedom, equality, democracy, happiness, and prosperity.

It was a time of extreme confusion. People didn't know what to believe in, whom to trust, or what direction to move in. This may be similar, in some ways, to the information age we live in today. We're constantly being bombarded with conflicting ideas through the media and the internet.

I searched for a mentor who could give me a clear answer on the correct way to live by reading a lot of books and holding discussions with friends. I was nineteen when I first met Mr. Toda. He compassionately and sincerely answered my questions. And he suggested that I set out on the path of Buddhism with the questing spirit of youth. I was deeply moved. I didn't understand the profound teachings of Buddhism at that time, but I was immediately drawn to Mr. Toda's character and personality.

Hearing that he had been persecuted and imprisoned for two years during the war for his beliefs, I was struck by his brave commitment to justice and peace. I instinctively felt I could place my trust in him.

Even now, when I think of Mr. Toda, I am uplifted and strength surges within me. No matter what hardships I encounter, I always greet them with a fighting spirit: "I am a disciple of Josei Toda. I am ready to take on anything!"

FJ: *A mentor makes it possible for youth to develop great strength.*

President Ikeda: Our feelings and emotions are constantly changing. One moment we may feel happy, the next sad; one moment enjoying ourselves, and the next filled with pain. This is especially true during one's youth.

Nichiren Daishonin cites the words "Become the master of your mind rather than let your mind master you" (WND-1, 502). It might seem fun to just do as we please all the time. But if we live our lives ruled by fleeting emotions, we will eventually lose our way. That's why it's so important to have a mentor whose guidance and example we can keep in our hearts as a spiritual compass.

Mr. Toda is always in my heart. To this day, I have an inner dialogue with him every day. I always ask myself what he'd do in my situation and what would make him proud. Because I have this inner foundation, I am never uncertain or afraid.

The path of mentor and disciple is the supreme path of human life. It is a path of justice and a path of hope. It is a path of happiness and victory.

> The path of mentor and disciple is *a path of happiness and victory.*

FJ: *Throughout history truly outstanding figures invariably had great mentors.*

President Ikeda: Yes. For example, the ancient Greek philosopher Plato had Socrates for a mentor. Martin Luther King Jr. had Benjamin Mays [president of Morehouse College, King's alma mater].

All the world leaders I have met had mentors whom they were indebted to. They were all great individuals who never forgot their gratitude to the mentors who contributed to their growth.

Genuine mentors seek to foster their disciples or students into capable individuals who go on to surpass them. Disciples who have a good mentor can awaken to and make full use of their innate strengths and abilities.

The renowned Indian poet and educator Rabindranath Tagore said, "Man knows himself as great where he sees great men."[71] Tagore also had a mentor when he was a student. I would like to dedicate those words of his to you, my young friends.

FJ: *Tagore was the first person from Asia to be awarded the Nobel Prize for Literature [in 1913]. You have received honorary doctorates from two universities in India that uphold Tagore's philosophy.[72] You have also met with former vice chancellor Bharati Mukherjee of Rabindra Bharati University, which started from Tagore's ancestral home.*

President Ikeda: Dr. Mukherjee was a highly respected educator and authority on Indian political philosophy. She was widowed at a young age and struggled as a single mother. But she continued to research and study Tagore's philosophy, something she continued throughout her life. She was truly a remarkable woman.

Unlikely as it may seem, Tagore wasn't very fond of studying when he was young. He was from a wealthy family and made to study with tutors, but the strict educational methods didn't suit him. For instance, whenever a tutor came to give a lesson, Tagore always found himself fighting off sleepiness or being easily distracted by music playing in the distance. He also pretended to be sick.

Rabindranath Tagore

Although the young Tagore did not enjoy studying, he had a gift for writing poetry. One of his schoolteachers realized this and asked Tagore to come see him. Tagore was afraid he was in trouble, so he was rather anxious when he walked into the teacher's room. But to his surprise, the teacher greeted him warmly, saying, "So, you write poetry?" and praised his work.

This teacher later brought Tagore to his most senior class and told him to recite his poetry in front of the students. When he did, everyone was astonished. They refused to believe that someone his age could write such fine poetry.[73] The presence of a teacher who recognized his ability was what allowed Tagore's talent to blossom.

After that, Tagore strove to perfect his art and went on to become a world-acclaimed poet. He also devoted himself to teaching others and even founded a school that produced many outstanding people. He believed that nothing was more important than cultivating character through human interaction.

Outstanding mentors raise outstanding disciples. Outstanding disciples later go on to become outstanding mentors to others. The path of mentor and disciple continues forever.

FJ: *During a dialogue with you, the well-known Japanese novelist Yasushi Inoue said: "In something you wrote earlier, you commented that, if you had not met Mr. Toda, you would not be the person you are. That kind of relation that existed between you two [is] the ideal one for teacher and disciple."*[74]

President Ikeda: I suffered from poor health when I was a boy. Because of the war, I couldn't attend school as much as I would have liked. My father had crippling rheumatism [leaving him unable to work]. My four older brothers were all sent off to war, and we didn't know when they would return. Even though I had tuberculosis, I worked hard to help support my family.

Then, thanks to Mr. Toda, I came to learn about Nichiren Buddhism and the correct way to live. As a result, I have lived a long and productive life. My mentor enabled me to develop my abilities and potential to the fullest.

To repay my profound gratitude to my mentor, I gave my all to assisting him while he was alive. After his passing, I devoted myself to serving the Soka Gakkai and its members, which he treasured more than anything.

Mr. Toda truly understood my heart, and I was deeply grateful to have him as my mentor. When Mr. Toda was going through the most difficult time, I expressed my vow as a disciple in a poem and gave it to him:

> *Still serving*
> *an old*
> *and mystic bond—*
> *though others change,*
> *I alter not.*

"Because our mentor-disciple relationship did not begin in this lifetime but was determined from the distant past, my heart will never change!" This was the sentiment I tried to convey, my commitment to strive forever with Mr. Toda. At that time, there were those who gave the outward appearance of being Mr. Toda's disciples. But they were not loyal to him in their hearts and ultimately ended up deserting him at a crucial moment.

Mr. Toda replied to my poem with one of his own:

> *Whenever I stand*
> *on the field of battle,*
> *you are the trusty sword*
> *I always keep*
> *at my side.*

"With you by my side, I need nothing more!" his words seemed to say. They electrified me. I vowed deep in my heart that I would strive alongside him as his trusty sword—acting as his right hand—throughout my life.

I have fulfilled all the promises I made to Mr. Toda. The mentors and disciples of the SGI have won! We have achieved great victories that will shine on into future generations.

Now, I have you, the future division members, to count on. I would like to share with you, my most beloved disciples, a poem that I once wrote for Soka schools students:

> **Nothing in this world**
> **is greater than the path**
> **of mentor and disciple.**
> **Never forget, my friends,**
> **these ties of victory.**

23

Nothing Is Impossible for Mentors and Disciples TOGETHER

Future Journal: *March is here, the spring month in which everything comes alive. Our future division members are also advancing toward the next stage of their lives. [In Japan, the school year ends in March and begins in April.]*

President Ikeda: To our graduates, many congratulations on your new departure! You've all worked hard. Please join me in a rousing cheer for yourselves as we look toward a bright future filled with hope.

For those of you who are moving on to the next grade, I hope you'll overflow with fresh determination and become shining examples for your juniors.

Some of you may be feeling discouraged because you didn't do as well as you had hoped in your school entrance examinations.[75] But by studying hard, you have been able to leave behind a proud history that will shine in your life as the crown of a genuine fighter.

There are times when, no matter how hard you try, things don't work out the way you wish. So instead of dwelling on the past, set your sights on the next challenge. That's what makes a true victor. Such people win in the end.

Overcoming sadness and hardship makes us stronger. We can develop greater character. Don't let setbacks keep you down forever. Hold your head up high and take a brave step forward!

> Instead of dwelling on the past, *set your sights on the next challenge*.

FJ: *Many members have sent in comments on the mentor-disciple relationship you discussed last time.*

Here are some: "Until now, I felt that the mentor-disciple relationship was hard to understand, but now I realize that it's actually something rooted in our daily lives."

"President Ikeda called us his 'most beloved disciples.' I was moved by how much trust he has in us."

"Even in the face of hardships, thinking of President Ikeda's high hopes enables me to continue striving because the bond of mentor and disciple exists between us. I'm not afraid of anything. I know I can win over any difficulty."

President Ikeda: I am so happy to hear that all of you are deepening your understanding of the mentor-disciple relationship. I talk with all of you in my heart every day. You are always in my thoughts when I am chanting.

You, the future division members, are my life. Even though we may be far apart and unable to meet in person, our lives are deeply connected. The Lotus Sutra says, "Those persons who had heard the Law dwelled here and there in various Buddha lands, constantly reborn in company with their teachers."[76] Mentors and disciples, joined by a vow for kosen-rufu, have promised to live out their lives and strive together for eternity.

Tsunesaburo Makiguchi and Josei Toda both deeply admired and studied the writings of the renowned American educator John Dewey. Dewey believed that the aim of education is endless growth, which in itself is happiness. Teachers and students should study and grow together. In other words, the mentor-disciple relationship lies at the core of education as well.

I have discussed Dewey's life and ideals with Dr. Larry Hickman and Dr. Jim Garrison, two American scholars who are carrying on the legacy of Dewey's philosophy. The mentor-disciple relationship was one of the major topics of our dialogue.

FJ: *Both men have served as presidents of the John Dewey Society in the United States. Dr. Garrison said: "Sharing an inquiry—or, in your terms, being on the same path— is very important. The mentor may be further along the path, but both are still bound in a profound unity."[77] And Dr. Hickman commented, "It is especially important to recall and celebrate the types of relationships that persist and that even grow in the face of crisis."[78]*

President Ikeda: The mentor-disciple relationship is the most fundamental path of life. In Buddhism, while mentor and disciple are different individuals, their hearts are one. They are also essentially equal. That is what is meant by the "oneness of mentor and disciple." Mentor and disciple are one in spirit. As such, they always advance together.

My mentor, Josei Toda, always highly valued the opinions of young people. He listened attentively to what they had to say. He deeply admired their serious seeking spirit. He often asked for my views: "Daisaku, what do you think? What's your opinion?" I was always very moved that he would put that much trust in an ordinary young man like myself. I was so grateful to have such a wonderful mentor.

John Dewey

Dewey declared: "Ours is the responsibility of conserving, transmitting, rectifying, and expanding the heritage of values we have received that those who come after us may receive it more solid and secure, more widely accessible and more generously shared than we have received it."[79] These words are engraved on his tombstone. Today, I would like to impart them to you, my successors and most beloved disciples.

Dr. Garrison has said that the SGI perfectly embodies and puts into practice this spirit described by Dewey.[80]

Though this may sound a bit difficult, the mentor provides the principles, and the disciples put them into practice. It is vital that the disciples continue to spread the mentor's principles exponentially, through their actions.

In my youth, I etched into my heart what I learned from Mr. Toda. I paid attention to everything he said, even things he said in just a lighthearted manner. Encouraging my fellow members, I dedicated myself to actualizing each one of my mentor's great visions, both in Japan and around the world.

FJ: Dewey also had a mentor whom he looked up to. At age fifteen, Dewey graduated from high school. He went on to university and postgraduate studies, where he majored in philosophy. There he met George S. Morris.

President Ikeda: Morris was a man of broad learning, yet he was not arrogant or conceited. He taught with sincerity and passion and explained things in a way that his students could easily understand.

Captivated by Morris's integrity, earnestness, and pleasant, outgoing personality, Dewey was inspired to study his hardest. Building on the foundation he received from him, Dewey was able to form a more widely accepted system of philosophy.

Dewey even named one of his children Morris, which shows how much he respected his teacher.

I wonder if you've ever heard of the expression "From the indigo, an even deeper blue" (WND-1, 457). It appears in the writings of Nichiren Daishonin. The indigo plant was used to dye fabric blue. Repeatedly soaking the material in the dye creates a deeper blue than the original dye. This expression also has the meaning of disciples surpassing the mentor.

To me, you are all my direct disciples who will go on to become "bluer than the indigo" (WND-1, 457) That's why I would like all of you to become strong, outstanding individuals no matter what. I hope all of you proudly make your way in the wide world. Because mentor and disciple are one, I have no doubt that you can achieve this.

My eternal message to you all is: "Nothing is impossible for Soka mentors and disciples. The spirit of the future division is to never give up. You can surely triumph!"

FJ: *One person shared: "I still don't deeply understand the mentor-disciple relationship, but when I'm feeling down, I read President Ikeda's books, chant, and decide to do what I can in my situation. That for me right now is the path of mentor and disciple."*

President Ikeda: That spirit is a source of joy and immense hope for me.

There are various things you can do in your daily lives as a disciple. For example, keep up your studies no matter the hardships, treasure your parents, build lifelong friendships, challenge yourselves to read books, study a foreign language, train your bodies and minds through sports and other such activities, and never accept bullying.

Basing yourself on chanting Nam-myoho-renge-kyo and challenging each task in front of you one after the other will lead to your victory. These victories will eventually give you the strength to open the way for the happiness of others and give you the wisdom to contribute to peace.

FJ: *A reader asks, "What does it mean for the mentor and disciple to be connected by Nam-myoho-renge-kyo?"*

President Ikeda: Right now [March 2014], the International Space Station, captained by the Japanese astronaut Koichi Wakata, is in orbit around Earth. Though far away, it communicates with Earth through radio waves. The waves sent by the transmitter are caught by the receiver. As long as the receiving side doesn't turn off its receiver, the waves will definitely be picked up. There is an undeniable connection, even though it is invisible.

The same kind of thing happens between people's hearts and lives. I continue chanting for you, the future division members, day after day, with faith in your great growth and victory.

Chanting creates the strongest "life waves" possible. As Nichiren Daishonin states: "There is nowhere throughout the worlds of the ten directions that the sound of our voices chanting [Nam-myoho-renge-kyo] do not reach."[81] With this in mind, I hope you'll also chant with faith in your own growth and victory. This is chanting with the shared spirit of mentor and disciple, by which our lives will definitely connect. So even if you lack self-confidence now, there's nothing to worry about. The "sun" of self-confidence is certain to rise in the hearts of those who try.

> *Chant with faith in your own growth and victory.*

The Daishonin teaches that if mentor and disciple are united in spirit, they can achieve anything. Mr. Toda had faith in me. And, in response, I worked my hardest. I told myself that, as Mr. Toda's disciple, nothing was impossible. I was able to overcome tuberculosis, which at that time was regarded as incurable. No obstacle could stop me. Everywhere I went, I created a record of victory as Mr. Toda's disciple.

Of course, when you're young, you may often feel anxious and uncertain. There may be times when you feel frustrated with who you are or find it hard to believe in yourself. That's perfectly fine. Because remember, I always believe in you more than anyone. I'm watching over you and praying wholeheartedly for you. Please advance cheerfully, with optimism and confidence.

Whatever the time or place, we can always have a dialogue in our hearts. Let's face every problem together, look forward with hope, and advance victoriously together!

I would like every one of you to make your youth a time full of delight and triumph. Please lead lives of happiness, overflowing with joy. This is the spirit of a mentor and my wish for all of you.

Each step you take will itself become the golden path of mentor and disciple.

Let's set forth! Let's walk the path to victory together!

Victory

Together

Mentor and Disciple

NOTES

Chapter 1: Let's Go Forward Together

1. Walt Whitman, "Song of the Open Road," *Leaves of Grass* (New York: Bantam Books, 1983), 123.
2. Whitman, *Leaves of Grass*, 132.
3. William Osler, *Aequanimitas: With Other Addresses to Medical Students, Nurses and Practitioners of Medicine* (Philadelphia: The Blakiston Company, 1904), 386.

Chapter 2: Let Your Unique Personality Shine!

4. Eiji Yoshikawa, *Musashi,* trans. Charles S. Terry (Tokyo: Kodansha International, 1981), 680.

Chapter 3: Friendship Is a Treasure

5. Daisaku Ikeda, *Journey of Life: Selected Poems of Daisaku Ikeda* (New York: I.B. Tauris & Co., Ltd., 2014), 7.
6. *The Analects of Confucius,* trans. Simon Leys (New York: W. W. Norton and Company, 1997), 59.
7. Hall Caine, *The Eternal City* (New York: D. Appleton and Company, 1901), 422.
8. Caine, *Eternal City,* 423.
9. Caine, *Eternal City,* 67.
10. Cicero, *Laelius, on Friendship; & The Dream of Scipio,* trans. J. G. F. Powell (Warminster, UK: Aris and Phillips Ltd., 1990), 39.

Chapter 4: Dreams Are the Key to Unlock a Brilliant Future

11. Translated from Japanese. Article in *Seikyo Shimbun,* June 12, 2005.
12. Translated from Japanese. Valentina Tereshkova-Nikolaeva, *Hateshinai Uchu e* (Into the boundless ocean of the universe), trans. Yoshiko Okada (Moscow: Progress Publishing, 1963), 134.

Chapter 5: Those Who Continue Learning Are Victors in Life

13. Translated from German. *Goethes gespräche: Gesamtausgabe* (Goethe's conversations: complete compilation), comp. Woldemar Frhr. von Biedermann, ed. Flodoard Frhr. von Biedermann (Leipzig: F. W. v. Biedermann, 1909), 2:10.
14. The dialogue was serialized in the Soka Gakkai–affiliated *Ushio* monthly magazine.
15. Translated from Japanese. Berta Schleicher, *Maruvida fon Maizenbuku* (Malwida von Meysenbug), trans. Toshihiko Katayama (Tokyo: Misuzu Shobo, 1957), 77–78.

16. Daisaku Ikeda, *A Youthful Diary: One Man's Journey From the Beginning of Faith to Worldwide Leadership for Peace* (Santa Monica, CA: World Tribune Press, 2001), 150.

Chapter 6: Keep Persevering With a Positive, Tenacious Attitude

17. Heinrich Schliemann, *Briefwechsel* (Correspondence), comp. and ed. Ernst Meyer (Berlin: Verlag Gebr. Mann, 1953), 1:121. (One of Schliemann's letters written in English.)

18. In a speech he delivered in January 7, 2001, President Ikeda wrote: "Schliemann visited Hachioji on June 19, 1865. It was during the period when Japan was undergoing its transition from the Edo period to the Meiji period. Schliemann later described his visit to Hachioji as having been particularly interesting. Writing of his impressions of this area, he said: 'Beautiful fields stretched in all directions. And the view from the hills was even more lovely.'"

19. Vincent Harding and Daisaku Ikeda, *America Will Be!* (Cambridge, MA: Dialogue Path Press, 2013), 190.

20. Translated from Japanese. Josei Toda, *Toda Josei zenshu* (Collected writings of Josei Toda) (Tokyo: Seikyo Shimbunsha, 1981), 1:282.

Chapter 7: Proudly Walk the Path of Self-Improvement

21. In Japan, school graduation takes place in March and the new school year, as well as the fiscal year, begins in April. School and university entrance exams take place from January to March.

22. Rainer Maria Rilke, *Letters to a Young Poet*, trans. Stephen Mitchell (New York: Vintage Books, 1986), 101.

23. Rilke, *Letters to a Young Poet*, 101.

Chapter 8: Having Appreciation for One's Parents

24. According to ninth- and tenth-century sources, the term originates from the custom of Buddhist teachers *(shi)* busily traveling around *(wasu)* to the homes of the laity to recite the sutras for them in the closing month of the year.

25. José Rizal National Centennial Commission, "Rizal as a Moral Leader," in *International Congress on Rizal, 4–8 December 1961: Data Papers / Commission on Science, Commission on Social Sciences, Commission on Humanities* (Manila: National Historical Institute, 1979), 278.

Chapter 9: The World Is Your Stage

26. See Daisaku Ikeda, "Education Toward Global Citizenship," *Soka Education: For the Happiness of the Individual*, Rev. Ed. (Santa Monica, CA: Middleway Press, 2015), 112–13.

27. Translated from Japanese. Inazo Nitobe, with commentary by Hitoshi Takeuchi, *Jibun o motto fukaku hore!: Nitobe Inazo no meicho "Yowatari no michi" o Yomu* (Cultivate yourself more deeply!: Reading Inazo Nitobe's famous work "The art of living") (Tokyo: Mikasa Shobo, 2006), 204.

Chapter 10: Leading a Victorious Youth Based on Chanting Nam-myoho-renge-kyo

28. In Japan, school graduation takes place in March and the new school year begins in April. School and university entrance exams take place from January to March.

29. From a letter dated May 26, 1994, addressed to President Ikeda from Dr. Lokesh Chandra, director of the International Academy of Indian Culture.

30. The lecture was titled "Toward a World Without War—Gandhism and the Modern World" and was given at the invitation of the Gandhi Smriti and Darshan Samiti (Gandhi Memorial Hall).

31. Mahatma Gandhi, *The Collected Works of Mahatma Gandhi, vol. 84, April 14, 1946–July 15, 1946* (New Delhi: The Publications Division, Ministry of Information and Broadcasting, Government of India, 1981), 379.

32. Mahatma Gandhi, *The Collected Works of Mahatma Gandhi, vol. 38, November 1928–February 1929* (New Delhi: The Publications Division, Ministry of Information and Broadcasting, Government of India, 1970), 248.

Chapter 11: You Can Do It!

33. In Japan, school graduation takes place in March and the new school year begins in April.

34. In Japan, junior high and high school each comprise three years of study.

35. The dialogue between Konosuke Matsuchita and Daisaku Ikeda was published as *Jinsei mondo* (Questions and answers about life); not translated into English.

36. Translated from Japanese. Konosuke Matsushita, *Matsushita Konosuke seiko no kingen 365* (Konosuke Matsushita—365 inspirational quotes for success) (Tokyo: PHP Kenkyusho, 2011), 232.

37. Matsushita, *Seiko no kingen 365*, 390.

Chapter 12: Challenge Yourselves and Grow

38. Rosa Parks, With Gregory J. Reed, *Dear Mrs. Parks: A Dialogue with Today's Youth* (New York: Lee and Low Books, Inc., 1996), 97.

39. Rosa Parks, *Dear Mrs. Parks*, 97.

40. Translated from Japanese. Tsunesaburo Makiguchi, *Makiguchi Tsunesaburo shingenshu* (Selected quotes of Tsunesaburo Makiguchi), ed. Takehisa Tsuji (Tokyo: Daisanbunmei-sha, 1979), 29.

Chapter 13: Shine Brightly and Illuminate the World!

41. Translated from French. Romain Rolland, *Journal des années de guerre: 1914–1919* (Journal of the war years: 1914–1919) (Paris: Albin Michel, 1952), 1325.

42. Romain Rolland, *Jean-Christophe in Paris*, trans. Gilbert Cannan (New York: Henry Holt and Company, 1911), 301.

43. Translated from French. Romain Rolland, *Le cloître de la Rue d'Ulm* (The cloister on the Rue d'Ulm) (Paris: Albin Michel, 1952), 74.

44. Rolland's friend was the French poet and critic André Suarès (1868–1948).

Chapter 14: Make Good Books Your Companions

45. Translated from Japanese. Anton Chekhov, *Chehofu no kotoba* (Words of Chekhov), trans. and ed. Seiro Sato (Tokyo: Yayoi Shobo, 1997), 25.
46. Anton Chekhov, *Plays*, trans. Elisaveta Fen (London: Penguin Books, 1954), 389.

Chapter 15: Having Courage and Compassion

47. The speech was titled "Radicalism Reconsidered" and delivered at Claremont McKenna College in 1993. Please see *My Dear Friends in America*, Third Edition (Santa Monica, CA: World Tribune Press, 2012), 222–32.
48. Leo Tolstoy, *Family Happiness: Stories* (New York: HarperCollins, 2009), 19.
49. Leo Tolstoy, *A Calendar of Wisdom*, trans. Peter Sekirin (New York: Scribner, 1997), 123.

Chapter 16: Sowing the Seeds of Peace

50. Daisaku Ikeda, *The Human Revolution* (Santa Monica, CA: World Tribune Press, 2004), 1:3.
51. Linus Pauling, *No More War!* (New York: Dodd, Mead and Company, 1962), 193.

Chapter 17: Peace Starts Where You Are

52. The Pugwash Conferences on Science and World Affairs was founded in 1957. Rotblat and the Pugwash Conferences were awarded the Nobel Peace Prize in 1995.
53. Joseph Rotblat and Daisaku Ikeda, *A Quest for Global Peace: Rotblat and Ikeda on War, Ethics, and the Nuclear Threat* (New York: I. B. Tauris, 2007), 32.
54. Rotblat and Ikeda, *A Quest for Global Peace*, 2.
55. "The Russell-Einstein Manifesto," http://www.pugwash.org/about/manifesto.htm (Accessed on January 31, 2014).
56. Elise Boulding and Daisaku Ikeda, *Into Full Flower: Making Peace Cultures Happen* (Cambridge, MA: Dialogue Path Press, 2010), 7.
57. Boulding and Ikeda, *Into Full Flower*, 10.
58. Daisaku Ikeda, *The New Human Revolution* (Santa Monica, CA: World Tribune Press, 1995), 1:1.

Chapter 18: Seeking Inspiration That Enriches the Heart

59. Translated from French. Pierre de Coubertin, "L'Amérique Universitaire" (The American university) in *Cosmopolis: An International Monthly Review*, ed. F. Ortmans (London: T. Fisher Unwin, 1897), 5:786.
60. Victor Hugo, *Les Misérables*, trans. Lee Fahnestock and Norman MacAfee (New York: Signet Classics, 2013), 217.
61. Translated from French. Victor Hugo, "Ce qui se passait aux Feuillantines" (What happened at the Feuillantines) in *Les Voix Intérieures; Les Rayons et les ombres* (Inner voices; sunlight and shadows) (Paris: Librairie Hachette, 1876), 225.
62. These diaries were published in English as *A Youthful Diary: One Man's Journey From the Beginning of Faith to Worldwide Leadership for Peace* (Santa Monica, CA: World Tribune Press, 2001).

Chapter 19: Envisioning a Hope-Filled Future Together

63. Wangari Muta Maathai, *Unbowed: A Memoir* (New York: Anchor Books, 2007), 70.

Chapter 20: Win With Nichiren's Writings

64. Daisaku Ikeda, *A Youthful Diary: One Man's Journey From the Beginning of Faith to Worldwide Leadership for Peace* (Santa Monica, CA: World Tribune Press, 2001), 49.
65. Ikeda, *A Youthful Diary*, 139.
66. The three bodies of the Buddha refer to the Dharma body, the reward body, and the manifested body. The Dharma body is the fundamental truth, or Law, to which a Buddha is enlightened. The reward body is the wisdom to perceive the Law. And the manifested body is the compassionate actions the Buddha carries out to lead people to happiness.

Chapter 21: Take a Courageous Step Toward the World Stage!

67. Nelson Mandela, *Long Walk to Freedom: The Autobiography of Nelson Mandela* (Boston: Little, Brown and Company, 1994), 544.
68. Mandela, *Long Walk to Freedom*, 544.
69. Nelson Mandela, *Conversations with Myself* (New York: Farrar, Straus and Giroux, 2010), 24.

Chapter 22: Nothing Is Greater Than the Path of Mentor and Disciple

70. In Japan, school graduation takes place in March and the new school year begins in April. School and university entrance exams take place from January to March.
71. Rabindranath Tagore, *Thoughts from Rabindranath Tagore* (London: Macmillan and Co., Ltd., 1929), 60.
72. President Ikeda received an honorary doctorate from Rabindra Bharati University in February 2004 and Visva-Bharati University in May 2006.
73. See Rabindranath Tagore, *My Reminiscences* (New York: The Macmillan Company, 1917), 49–50.
74. Daisaku Ikeda and Yasushi Inoue, *Letters of Four Seasons,* trans. Richard L. Gage (Tokyo: Kodansha International Ltd., 1980), 44.

Chapter 23: Nothing Is Impossible for Mentors and Disciples Together

75. In Japan, school and university entrance exams take place from January to March.
76. *The Lotus Sutra and Its Opening and Closing Sutras,* trans. Burton Watson (Tokyo: Soka Gakkai, 2009), 178.
77. Jim Garrison, Larry Hickman, and Daisaku Ikeda, *Living as Learning: John Dewey in the 21st Century* (Cambridge, MA: Dialogue Path Press, 2014), 36.
78. Garrison, Hickman, and Ikeda, *Living as Learning*, 35.
79. John Dewey, *A Common Faith* (New Haven: Yale University Press, 1934), 87.
80. Garrison, Larry, and Ikeda, *Living as Learning*, 41.
81. Nichiren, *Gosho zenshu* (Tokyo: Soka Gakkai, 1952), 808. From "Oko Kikigaki" (The recorded lectures); not included in WND, vols. 1 and 2.